Martin Scorsese's *Raging Bull*

Raging Bull has been called the greatest film of the 1980s, the greatest box-ing film ever made, and one of the greatest films of all time. This volume provides a timely critical appreciation of this work. In his introduction, Kevin J. Hayes recounts how the story of Jake La Motta, the protagonist in *Raging Bull*, came to be made into a film. He examines the film through the oeuvre of Martin Scorsese, traces its sources, and positions it within the history of cinema. Subsequent chapters examine *Raging Bull* from a variety of methodological and critical perspectives and lend new in-sights into the work. Aimed for use in undergraduate and graduate film courses, *Martin Scorsese's "Raging Bull"* will also enhance appreciation of this seminal film for general audiences.

Kevin J. Hayes is professor of English at the University of Central Oklahoma. A scholar of American literature and cinema, he is the au-thor of several books, including *Poe and the Printed Word* and *An American Cycling Odyssey, 1887.*

CAMBRIDGE FILM HANDBOOKS

General Editor: *Andrew Horton, University of Oklahoma*

Each CAMBRIDGE FILM HANDBOOK is intended to focus on a single film from various theoretical, critical, and contextual perspectives. This "prism" approach is designed to give students and general readers valuable background and insight into the cinematic, artistic, cultural, and sociopolitical importance of individual films by including essays by leading film scholars and critics. Furthermore, these handbooks are meant to help the reader better grasp the nature of the critical and theoretical discourse on cinema as an art form, as a visual medium, and as a cultural product. Filmographies and selected bibliographies are added to help the reader to continue his or her own exploration of the film under consideration.

Martin Scorsese's
Raging Bull

Edited by

KEVIN J. HAYES
University of Central Oklahoma

CAMBRIDGE
UNIVERSITY PRESS

PUBLISHED BY THE PRESS SYNDICATE OF THE UNIVERSITY OF CAMBRIDGE
The Pitt Building, Trumpington Street, Cambridge, United Kingdom

CAMBRIDGE UNIVERSITY PRESS
The Edinburgh Building, Cambridge CB2 2RU, UK
40 West 20th Street, New York, NY 10011-4211, USA
477 Williamstown Road, Port Melbourne, VIC 3207, Australia
Ruiz de Alarcón 13, 28014 Madrid, Spain
Dock House, The Waterfront, Cape Town 8001, South Africa

http://www.cambridge.org

First published 2005

Printed in the United States of America

Typefaces ITC Stone Serif 9.5/13.5 pt. and Gill Sans   *System* LaTeX 2_ε [TB]

A catalog record for this book is available from the British Library.

Library of Congress Cataloging in Publication Data
Martin Scorsese's Raging bull/edited by Kevin J. Hayes.
    p.   cm. – (Cambridge film handbooks)
    Filmography: p.
    Includes bibliographical references and index.
    ISBN 0-521-82915-1 – ISBN 0-521-53604-9 (pbk.)
    1. Raging bull (Motion picture)   2. Scorsese, Martin – Criticism and
interpretation.   I. Hayes, Kevin J.   II. Cambridge film handbooks series.
PN1997.R2253M37   2004
791.43′72 – dc22   2004048597

ISBN 0 521 82915 1 hardback
ISBN 0 521 53604 9 paperback

Contents

List of Illustrations

List of Contributors

TODD BERLINER is Associate Professor and Chair of the Department of Film Studies at the University of North Carolina at Wilmington. His essays have appeared in *Film Quarterly, Cinema Journal, Journal of Film and Video, Style*, and *Quarterly Review of Film and Video*. He is currently completing a book entitled *Stylistic Perversity in Hollywood Cinema: American Films of the 1970s*.

LEGER GRINDON is Professor of Film Studies and the Director of the Film and Media Culture Program at Middlebury College in Vermont. He is the author of *Shadows on the Past: Studies in the Historical Fiction Film* (1994). His essays and reviews have appeared in periodicals such as *Cinema Journal, Film Quarterly, Cineaste, Film History*, and *Velvet Light Trap*. He is currently working on a book on Hollywood boxing films.

KEVIN J. HAYES is Professor of English at the University of Central Oklahoma, where he teaches courses on literature, film, and folklore. His books include *Folklore and Book Culture* (1997); *The Library of William Byrd of Westover* (1997), for which he won the first annual Virginia Library History Award; *Melville's Folk Roots* (1999); *Poe and the Printed Word* (Cambridge University Press, 2000); and *An American Cycling Odyssey, 1887* (2002). His essays on film have appeared in such periodicals as *Cinema Journal, Film Criticism, Studies in European Cinema, Studies in French Cinema*, and *Visible Language*. He is currently working on a book about Charlie Chaplin.

PEGGY McCORMACK is Professor of English and Director of the Film Program at Loyola University in New Orleans, where she teaches courses in American literature and film. She has published *The Rule of Money: Gender, Class and Exchange Economics in the Fiction of Henry James* (1990), edited *Questioning the Master: Gender and Sexuality in Henry James's Writing* (2000), and contributed to *Henry James Goes to the Movies* (2002). She is presently working on a book to be titled *"Neo, You Are the One": Technique, Rhetoric, and Gender in American Cinema.*

MARK NICHOLLS is Lecturer in Cinema Studies in the School of Art History, Cinema, Classical Studies and Archaeology at the University of Melbourne, Australia. His areas of teaching and research include psychoanalysis, Italian national cinemas, art house cinema, Hollywood melodrama, and Australian television. In addition to his monograph, *Scorsese's Men: Melancholia and the Mob* (2004), he has contributed to *Metro, Australian Screen Education*, and *Journal of Film and Video* and chapters in various edited collections. He lectures in the Screen Education Program at the Australian Centre for the Moving Image and is a regular film reviewer on ABC radio in Australia.

MICHAEL PETERSON is an assistant professor of Theater and Drama at the University of Wisconsin, where he teaches courses in theater research, performance studies, and popular performance. He is the author of *Straight White Male* (1997), a critique of identity privilege in monologues by performance artists and comedians. His current project is an interdisciplinary study called "Las Vegas Culture."

Abbreviations

Kelly   Kelly, Mary Pat. *Martin Scorsese: A Journey*. New York: Thunder's Mouth Press, 1996.

MSI   Scorsese, Martin. *Martin Scorsese: Interviews*. Ed. Peter Brunette. Jackson: University Press of Mississippi, 1999.

SS   Scorsese, Martin. *Scorsese on Scorsese*. Ed. David Thompson and Ian Christie. London: Faber and Faber, 1989.

Introduction

The Heritage and Legacy of *Raging Bull*

Martin Scorsese's *Raging Bull* (1980) represents American filmmaking at its best. Since its initial release, the film has garnered a significant critical reputation. It has been called the greatest film of the 1980s, the greatest boxing film ever made, the greatest sports film ever made, and, indeed, one of the greatest films of all time. Superlatives abound whenever people talk about *Raging Bull*. Not only is it an exemplary cinematic work, it is also a cultural icon representing a rich cross section of themes, issues, and characters that reflect American culture in ways that typical Hollywood films do not. Furthermore, *Raging Bull* is a highly personal film. It reflects Scorsese's unique personal vision, captures the personality of the brutal but all-too-human Jake La Motta, and perpetuates the intimate working relationship between Scorsese and his star Robert De Niro.

Around the time Scorsese was making *Alice Doesn't Live Here Anymore* (1974), De Niro gave him a copy of *Raging Bull*, the autobiography of Jake La Motta, which La Motta co-wrote with Joseph Carter, a miscellaneous writer, and Peter Savage, a longtime friend who figures prominently in the book as Pete, a partner in Jake's early criminal activities and in his subsequent success in boxing. Later becoming acquainted with Savage, Scorsese found him to be "an amazing character." Scorsese generally enjoyed reading La Motta's autobiography, but it seemed to him that Savage was most responsible for its content. Discussing Savage's influence on the book, Scorsese observed, "He put a dramatic structure on Jake's chaotic existence. It wasn't so

I

much Jake speaking about himself as Pete explaining Jake to Jake!" (*MSI*, 85).

De Niro, of course, presented the book hoping that Scorsese would adapt it for the cinema and that he would cast him in the lead. The work appealed to De Niro because it contained what he called "some good scenes," meaning scenes with "dramatic possibilities, and irony, and humor, and something that people can relate to" (Kelly, 122–123). In the book, Jake is a despicable character, but De Niro did not see Jake's despicability as a barrier to bringing his story to the cinema. Early in the book, Jake apparently beats a man to death, commits several robberies, and rapes a young woman. None of these episodes deterred De Niro's enthusiasm for the project.

La Motta's autobiography does possess cinematic sensibilities. In the book, motion pictures give Jake a means of interpreting his personal past. Throughout the narrative, Jake uses film analogies to explain his actions. He compares the act of remembering his past to "looking at an old black-and-white movie . . . a string of poorly lit sequences, some of them with no beginning and some with no end." Recalling a robbery he and Pete attempted, he compares their physical movements to those of "movie soldiers walking very carefully over some terrain, afraid of stepping on land mines." To stop Jake from brazenly challenging some local hoods at one point in the story, Pete yells, "Now listen, you're not in some goddam gangster movie, so don't act stupid." Taking Pete to the hospital after he has been shot, Jake finds that the emergency ward "was fast and efficient the way it is in the movies."[1]

Whereas Scorsese would end Jake's story with him practicing his stage routine in the dressing room of the Barbizon Plaza, the autobiography continues the story beyond this point in Jake's life. Around the time of his performance at the Barbizon, Jake was starting to get some dramatic roles on stage, on television, and in films. Pete, amazingly enough, had become a filmmaker himself. Directing and producing a film entitled *A House in Naples* (1970), Pete cast Jake in a leading part. In his closing pages, Jake mentions some additional dramatic roles he played, without mentioning a small part he had in a major film: Jake plays the bartender who dispenses drinks to Paul Newman and Piper Laurie in *The Hustler* (1961).

Shortly before describing his budding career as a stage performer and movie actor in the autobiography, Jake relates a low point in his life. After leaving Miami and returning to New York, he eventually became so broke that he was forced to work on a maintenance crew in Central Park. Being between wives, he was living in a crummy hotel room and, with little else to do, he amused himself by reading all the paperbacks he could find. The volumes on this urban pugilist's book-shelf apparently included Robert Ardrey's *The Territorial Imperative*, one of the few books Jake specifically mentions by title.[2] It is hard to say whether Jake really read *The Territorial Imperative* at this point in his life. He could have. The book was widely available in cheap paperback editions, and it was translated into many languages. Film enthusiasts may recognize it as the book Jean Yanne reads to Mireille Darc in Jean-Luc Godard's *Week-end* (1967).

The reference to *The Territorial Imperative* within La Motta's au-tobiography seems so appropriate that it may reflect Peter Savage's shaping hand more than Jake's actual reading tastes. One of those pseudoscientific works that occasionally capture the popular imagi-nation, *The Territorial Imperative* emphasizes the instinctual basis of human behavior and offers numerous parallels between man and an-imal. Man, like his animal ancestors, requires the possession of ter-ritory to fulfill his most basic needs. In the passage Godard quoted in *Week-end*, for example, the hippopotamus marks its territory with fecal matter, which it disperses with its tail. Performing a private activity within the collective space of a pond, the hippo reveals its acceptance of collective behavior. Despite the popularity of *The Territorial Imperative*, serious readers scoffed at Ardrey's ideas when it appeared, and the book has been all but forgotten now. Situated within the life story of a boxer known as a raging bull, however, Ardrey's ideas about man's instinctual animal-like nature retain a strange relevance.

De Niro's presentation copy of *Raging Bull* did not immediately convince Scorsese to undertake a film adaptation of La Motta's story. At first, Scorsese was unconvinced that a film version of the book was feasible or, for that matter, desirable. Besides, he and De Niro had two other films already planned for the coming years, *Taxi Driver* (1976) and *New York, New York* (1977). Still, Scorsese did not reject the idea outright. Perhaps the clearest indication that the *Raging Bull* project remained a possibility is the repeated appearance of Peter Savage on Scorsese's set. Savage even finagled himself into the cast of two films. In *Taxi Driver*, he plays The John, and in *New York, New York*, he plays Horace Morris's assistant.

The disappointing reception of *New York, New York*, a film Scorsese poured his heart into, put him into a blue funk. As an homage to the Hollywood musical, *New York, New York* pleased genuine cinema aficionados, but it disappointed many of the fans Scorsese had gained with such works as *Mean Streets* (1973) and *Taxi Driver*, viewers who had no nostalgia for the New York of decades past and preferred a grittier image of the city, complete with, in Travis Bickle's words, whores, skunk pussies, buggers, queens, fairies, dopers, and junkies. *Raging Bull*, Scorsese came to realize, would allow him to return to the world he had created in *Mean Streets* and *Taxi Driver*. Eventually, he came to see *Raging Bull* as completing a cycle he had started with *Mean Streets*.[3]

Shrewdly, De Niro also presented a copy of *Raging Bull* to Mardik Martin, an old friend of Scorsese's since their film school days at NYU with whom he had collaborated on *Mean Streets*. Despite Scorsese's hesitance, Martin began turning La Motta's autobiography into a screenplay. Martin spent two years researching and writing different versions of the story, but not he, De Niro, Scorsese, or producer Irwin Winkler were satisfied with the results. "When Mardik came in with *Raging Bull*," Scorsese recalled, "it was like *Rashomon*. He got twenty-five versions of the story because all the characters were alive."[4]

Martin was quietly relieved when Winkler took him off the project. He handed all of his various drafts and research materials to Paul Schrader, who reshaped Martin's disparate materials into something close to a final version of the screenplay. Most importantly, Schrader was responsible for the film's basic structure: he was the one who, in Scorsese's words, "had the idea of opening with the speech on the stage and linking that with Jake's first defeat, in Cleveland" (*MSI*, 88).

Even after Schrader completed his script there were still parts of it that the others, especially Winkler, found dissatisfying. Schrader had written what he called "one of the best soliloquies I ever wrote, a two- or three-page masturbation monologue, which happens when

1. "I am not an animal."

Jake is in his jail cell. It was to be the climax of the film. La Motta is trying to masturbate and talking to himself, conjuring up images of the women he's known. He manages to get an erection and then he remembers how terribly he treated people and can't manage to masturbate. Finally, he blames his hand, and smashes his hand against the cell wall" (Kelly, 124). Speaking of this scene, Scorsese said, "On paper it was beautiful, but how do you shoot it?"[5] (Figure 1) Scorsese and De Niro decided to rework the script themselves. To that end, they traveled to St. Martin, where they spent three weeks hammering out a final working script. De Niro recalled, "Marty and I liked parts of Schrader's script but not others. We still had to make it our own. So we revised the script, and went over each scene, sometimes adding dialogue" (Kelly, 126).

Once Scorsese was committed to the project, De Niro began his rigorous physical training for the role. Scorsese filmed a few of his training sessions in 8 mm and, as he tells the story, happened to show them to Michael Powell. The director of *The Red Shoes* (1948) found the appearance of De Niro's red boxing gloves distracting. Powell helped Scorsese realize that, for most adults, memories of boxing were black-and-white memories (*MSI*, 84). Scorsese's decision to film *Raging Bull* in black and white partly stems from his desire to re-create such boxing memories. His growing dissatisfaction with color film stock also helped persuade him to make the film black and white.

Scorsese named these two reasons as the ones that convinced him to shoot *Raging Bull* in black and white.[6] There are others. Few can deny the influence of cinematographer Michael Chapman. La Motta's comparison between the memories of his personal past and a black-and-white movie in the autobiography offers another precedent, though Scorsese has denied La Motta's influence in this regard (*MSI*, 84). The photography of *Life* magazine also influenced *Raging Bull*, as Eleanor Ringel noticed. She called Cathy Moriarty "a Lana Turnerish blonde with the sultry, sun-baked appeal of the '40s *Life* magazine cover."[7] Furthermore, black-and-white allowed Scorsese to distinguish his boxing film from the numerous others that were appearing in the wake of *Rocky* (1976). In an era when color films were the norm, the choice of black and white was a conscious aesthetic choice, which gave a film an artistic aura. Recall some of the black-and-white films that had appeared during the preceding decade – *The Last Picture Show* (1971), *Lenny* (1974), and *Manhattan* (1979).

Production on *Raging Bull* began as De Niro's conditioning reached its peak. Once the early parts of the film were shot and the fight scenes completed, production shut down so that its star could travel to Italy and load up on pasta to prepare himself for the later parts of the film. De Niro returned from his eating binge to shoot the Pelham Parkway sequences, but then he went back to Italy for more linguine.

De Niro's excessive weight gain became the most publicized fact about the film's production. Upon its release, nearly all the contemporary reviewers mentioned it. The remarks of British reviewers were especially apt. Commenting on De Niro's weight gain, Peter Ackroyd observed, "The man without a soul has nowhere to go but outward. This quick change obesity adds a further note of authenticity to a film which already has that quality in excess."[8] Reviewing the film for *The New Statesman*, John Coleman went on about De Niro's weight gain at some length:

> To impersonate this unprepossessing oaf, Scorsese's favourite actor Robert De Niro became literally a glutton for punishment, putting on some 60 lb. of flab. Watching his La Motta physically deteriorate between the years 1941 and 1964 is an awe-inspiring experience, and likely to be a one-off in cinema history. (A mean voice whispers

we may yet witness the first Academy Award for Forced Feeding.) But De Niro is, of course, more than the sum of his swelling, bloated parts and what he gives here is certainly a performance as well, in its awful, dumb stillnesses before unbridled violence, in the painful precision of its self-pity, in the boozy crumminess of the later years, when the champ's occupation's gone and he tells cheap jokes into a mike.[9]

Coleman, of course, was wrong about De Niro's weight gain being a one-off in cinema history. Since *Raging Bull*, the willingness to gain weight for a part has become a mark of an actor's dedication to the role. Recently, Charlize Theron put on considerable weight to portray serial killer Aileen Wuornos in *Monster* (2003). Speaking of Theron's Oscar-winning performance, one reviewer commented that not since *Raging Bull* "has there been a transformation this powerful and effective."[10]

Not all of the contemporary reviewers appreciated *Raging Bull*, but almost all of them recognized it as a work of great power. Reviewing the film for *Maclean's*, the Toronto weekly, Lawrence O'Toole observed, "Scorsese has captured what Norman Mailer described in *The Fight* as 'the carnality of boxing,' the 'meat against meat,' and has flayed the genre at the same time. The movies that de-romanticized boxing in the past – *The Harder They Fall, Requiem for a Heavyweight* – always gave the audience something to hold onto: the fighter's humanity. Scorsese doesn't." Like many viewers, O'Toole was hypnotized by its imagery despite the repulsiveness of its protagonist. He concluded, "It's unpleasant, he's unpleasant, and we can't stop watching."[11]

Boxing has captured the American imagination and served as a fit subject for creative treatment since the time before motion pictures. A number of different literary works depict boxing matches but perhaps no work does so with more verve than "The Fight" – not the book by Norman Mailer but the short story by Augustus Baldwin Longstreet, which Edgar Allan Poe called "a sketch unsurpassed in dramatic vigor."[12] A classic of American literature, "The Fight" depicts a contest that adumbrates the Jake La Motta–Tony Janiro fight in *Raging Bull*. In the film, Joey (Joe Pesci) says that Jake knocked

Janiro's nose "from one side of his face to the other." And Tommy Como (Nicholas Colasanto), describing Janiro's appearance at the end of the fight, uttered the film's most memorable line: "He ain't pretty no more." Describing Billy Stallions, one of Longstreet's contestants, one spectator observes, "He hit the ground so hard, it jarred his nose off. Now ain't he a pretty man as he stands! He shall have my sister Sall just for his pretty looks. I want to get in the breed of them sort o' men, to drive ugly out of my kin folks."[13]

Though the verbal parallels between "The Fight" and *Raging Bull* suggest a continuity between the two works, Scorsese's debt to the literary tradition is relatively slight compared to his debt to the history of cinema. True, *Mean Streets* does make multiple allusions to Shakespeare's *Julius Caesar*, but Scorsese's obsession with the cinema has meant that he has been likelier to get his literary references through the intermediary of film. But like the finest literary works, *Raging Bull* presents an elaborate tissue of references and allusions that significantly enhance its complexity.

Consider the final shot of the last fight between Jake La Motta and Sugar Ray Robinson in *Raging Bull*, which displays a close-up of one of the ring ropes dripping with blood. Describing the inspiration for this shot to an interviewer, Scorsese traced it to the recent boxing matches he had attended as part of his research for the film: "The first evening, even though I was far away from the ring, I saw the sponge red with blood, and the film started to take form. The next time, I was much closer, and I saw the blood dripping from the ropes. I said to myself that this sure didn't have anything to do with sport!" (*MSI*, 95). Scorsese has related this anecdote multiple times to different interviewers, but it has not appreciably changed in the retelling. What he has withheld from his interviewers is that there was another, and perhaps more important, influence on this image, which he modeled on a shot from *Toby Dammit* (1968). Federico Fellini's adaptation of Poe's short story, "Never Bet the Devil Your Head," *Toby Dammit* also influenced *The Last Temptation of Christ* (1988), as Scorsese has freely admitted (*SS*, 143).

At the end of *Toby Dammit*, Terence Stamp, in his role as Fellini's title character, attempts to drive a new Ferrari over a chasm. Unknown to him, a taut wire extends across the roadway. As he reaches the wire, it decapitates him. Fellini does not show the decapitation, but after the fact he shows a close-up of a section of the wire dripping with blood.

Wildly departing from the Poe tale on which it is based, *Toby Dammit* tells the story of a popular British actor who comes to Italy to star in what he is told will be the first Catholic Western. The priest who tells him this is also the film's producer. Once the two meet at the airport, the priest explains the concept of the film to Toby. It will have what his friend Roland Barthes might call a syntagmatic structure: it will be "something between Dreyer and Pasolini with a soupçon of John Ford." The priest's words are not inappropriate to *Raging Bull*. The combination of classic Hollywood filmmaking and elements of European art cinema has appealed to Scorsese since the start of his career. A rich mosaic of film references, *Raging Bull* itself draws on the history of cinema to tell its story.

During its production, Scorsese feared that *Raging Bull* would be his last feature film. Consequently, he decided to put into it everything he could, everything that he knew and felt (*SS*, 77). He explicitly admitted this inclusiveness after the completion of *Raging Bull*, but the film itself, which contains recognizable references to numerous films, implies as much. The image of De Niro shadowboxing in his hooded robe during the opening credit sequence, as Amy Taubin has recognized, recalls one of Rossellini's monks in *The Flowers of St. Francis* (1950).[14] Up-ending a dinner table early in the film, De Niro performs a gesture reminiscent of an action performed by Paul Scofield in Peter Brook's *King Lear* (1971). The appearance of Cathy Moriarty adorned in a snood echoes the image of Ginger Rogers in her snood toward the end of *The Major and the Minor* (1942). The shot of the organist at the end of one fight in *Raging Bull* is framed similarly to shots of the organist at the hockey arena in *Slap Shot* (1977). Scorsese's use of still photography, point-of-view shots, slow motion, and intermittent flash bulbs during the fight sequences in *Raging Bull* recalls the opening fight sequence in *Requiem for a Heavyweight* (1962).

A reference to another film functions effectively as Scorsese's admission that he was putting everything into *Raging Bull* he could. Depicting the aging, overweight Jake La Motta in his dressing room prior to a stage performance, Robert De Niro ends a verse recitation with a traditional saying: "That's entertainment!" Though a proverbial expression common to the realm of show business, these words also happened to form the title of an unexpectedly popular film released a half dozen years earlier, *That's Entertainment* (1974), a retrospective documenting the classical Hollywood musical. Presented as a pastiche of clips from famous MGM musicals, *That's Entertainment* effectively eulogized the genre.[15] The allusion to this film suggests that *Raging Bull*, too, can be seen as a pastiche of references to earlier films.

Naturally, *Raging Bull* owes an important debt to the heritage of the boxing film genre. Take Buster Keaton's *Battling Butler* (1926), for example. Scorsese has called Keaton "the only person who had the right attitude about boxing in the movies for me" (*SS*, 80). It is not hard to see what lured Scorsese to *Battling Butler*. Much that can be said about Keaton's boxing film applies to Scorsese's. As the opening credits end, *Battling Butler* depicts a close-up of a bell, which clangs to start a round of boxing. After this shot, however, the film does not cut to a boxing match; rather, it cuts to a stately mansion where the film's story begins. As Scorsese would more than a half century later, Keaton deliberately paralleled the cinema with the boxing arena.

Attending a boxing match as a spectator, Keaton, in his dandified role as Alfred Butler, happens to sit next to the manager of a boxer named Alfred "Battling" Butler. The manager cannot watch the fight without mimicking the punches of the boxers he sees. The kind of behavior the manager exemplifies would become a commonplace of the boxing film. Consider the numerous shots of the crowd Robert Wise included in *The Set-Up* (1949). Depicting such violence among the spectators, Keaton anticipated the violence among the spectators in the first fight sequence of *Raging Bull*. Both Keaton and Scorsese recognized the boxing ring as a microcosm revealing the violence endemic to modern society.

As part of this violent world, Keaton also depicted violence against women. When "Battling" Butler sees his wife enter a hotel room with Keaton, he charges into the room to confront them. Keaton manages to sneak away, but as he listens to what is happening after his escape, he hears a light bulb shatter, a sound symbolizing the violence occurring behind the hotel room's closed door. When the wife appears the next morning, she has a big black eye. Keaton refrained from showing the intervening violence. Scorsese, on the other hand, would depict what Keaton had ellipted, the domestic scenes where so much disturbing violence occurs.

2. One inspiration: Glen Ford in *The Big Heat* (1953).

In terms of both genre and visual style, film noir deserves recognition as another important influence on *Raging Bull*. Discussing the cinematic heritage of the film, Scorsese admits the importance of one particular film noir, *Force of Evil* (1948). "*Force of Evil* was a great influence on me," he has explained, "because of the relationship between the brothers, showing what happened in the course of betrayal, and that strange dialogue written in verse" (*SS*, 78). On other occasions, Scorsese has reinforced how much *Force of Evil* has influenced him. He included the work in "Martin Scorsese Presents," a series of videotapes that also included *Pursued* (1947), which Scorsese identified in his introduction as the first noir western – an identification that shows how he enjoys films that mix different genres. Scorsese further appreciated *Force of Evil* in *A Personal Journey with Martin Scorsese Through American Movies* (1998).

When it comes to the influence of film noir, as in the case of *Toby Dammit*, what Scorsese has not admitted may be as important as what he has. Though Scorsese's collected interviews do not mention it, Fritz Lang's *The Big Heat* (1953) is one film noir that significantly shaped the visual style of *Raging Bull*. Playing a police detective in search of his wife's killer, Glen Ford visits a junkyard in one _similar to 'Waterfront'?_

sequence and interviews a brave old woman who has gone behind her boss's back to speak with him. The interview takes place through a chainlink fence. Lang depicts their conversation in a traditional shot/reverse shot sequence, but each actor speaks through the fence, a symbolic representation of the figurative prisons in which they find themselves (Figure 2). When Jake first meets Vickie (Cathy Moriarty), they, too, speak through a chainlink fence. Scorsese borrowed from Lang to show both Jake and Vickie trapped on opposite sides of the fence (Figure 3).

Though beholden to the boxing film and film noir, _Raging Bull_ may be less indebted to any particular genre or visual style than to a handful of individual filmmakers. Fritz Lang, for instance, gave Scorsese a filmmaker with a background in European cinema who came to America and, working in Hollywood, created some of his greatest works. In the classification scheme Scorsese devised for _A Personal Journey_, Lang was a smuggler, that is, a director who worked within the Hollywood system but who managed to incorporate aesthetic elements characteristic of his own unique, personal vision.

Samuel Fuller, who falls into a different category – the iconoclast – also exerted an important influence on _Raging Bull_. Interviewed for _The Typewriter, the Rifle and the Movie Camera_ (1996), an appreciative documentary of Fuller's life and work, Scorsese explained that he deliberately modeled one of the fight scenes in _Raging Bull_ on a scene from Fuller's _Steel Helmet_ (1951), arguably the greatest Korean war film ever made. _Raging Bull_ also owes a debt to what many consider Fuller's finest work, _Shock Corridor_ (1963). In this largely black-and-white film, Fuller incorporated brief color sequences. Each reflects a subjective mental state of the film's psychologically disturbed characters yet precedes a temporary moment of mental clarity. Similarly, the color footage of home movies in _Raging Bull_ depicts traditional and widely accepted behavior – courtship, marriage, parenthood – that represents moments of calm in an otherwise violent and disturbing world.

Jean-Luc Godard is another filmmaker who has exerted an important influence on Scorsese. _Taxi Driver_ contains Scorsese's most well-known Godard allusion, the extreme close-up of Travis Bickle's glass of Alka-Seltzer echoing the extreme close-up of a cup of coffee in

3. Like a tiger in a cage.

Two or Three Things I Know About Her (1967). Others can be identified. The hotel bedroom scene between Charlie (Harvey Keitel) and
Teresa (Amy Robinson) in *Mean Streets*, for one, recalls the lengthy
hotel bedroom scene in *Breathless* (1960). *Raging Bull* seems more
indebted to *Contempt* (1963), a film Scorsese would continue to appreciate. The soundtrack of *Casino* (1995) directly refers to *Contempt*
and, in 1997, Scorsese personally sponsored the theatrical re-release
of Godard's film. Interrogating Vickie regarding her whereabouts one
evening, Jake echoes the behavior of Paul Javal (Michel Piccoli), who
similarly questions his wife Camille (Brigitte Bardot) regarding her
whereabouts in *Contempt*.

Beyond the impact of specific works, Godard influenced Scorsese
in a more general way, too. In 1972, *Godard on Godard*, a collection
of the filmmaker's critical essays, appeared in English translation.
Discussing *Two or Three Things I Know About Her*, Godard explained,
"During the course of the film – in its discourse, its discontinuous
course, that is – I want to include everything, sport, politics, even
groceries.... Everything can be put into a film. Everything should
be put into a film."[16] These words are remarkably similar to those
Scorsese would use to describe his efforts to put everything he knew
and felt into *Raging Bull*. Godard offered an example of a filmmaker
who did not hold back, and when it came to *Raging Bull*, Scorsese
most certainly did not hold back.

Raging Bull received numerous accolades upon its release. It was nominated for eight Academy Awards. Robert De Niro won the Oscar for Best Actor, and Thelma Schoonmaker won for Best Editing. De Niro also won the Golden Globe for Best Acting and earned further Best Acting awards from the Boston Society of Film Critics (BSFC), the Los Angeles Film Critics Association, the National Board of Review, and the New York Film Critics Circle. Appreciation of Joe Pesci in the role of Jake La Motta's brother Joey was well-nigh universal. He received numerous acting awards, including the British Academy Award for Most Outstanding Newcomer to Leading Film Role. Michael Chapman received the BSFC Award for Best Cinematography and a similar award from the National Society of Film Critics, which also named Scorsese Best Director.

Raging Bull has been the subject of numerous critical essays, and it has also received attention beyond the realm of film studies. Classical scholar Carlin Barton, in a challenging new interpretation of Roman gladiator contests, used *Raging Bull* for comparison. Traditionally, the gladiator has been seen as a symbol of decadent Rome, but Barton argued that in the arena the gladiator was "removed temporarily from the tawdry toiling and moiling of political life. As in the bullfight or the boxing ring, victory can be of a simplicity, purity, and splendor never achieved outside the limited perimeter of the arena." The arena "offered a stage on which might be reenacted a lost set of sorely lamented values." *Raging Bull*, according to Barton, constitutes "a brilliant modern artistic portrayal of a similar phenomenon": "Outside the arena struggle was complex, tainted, sordid, unclear. Inside, though severe and dangerous, the rewards were a sense of purity and valor and honor."[17]

Perhaps the most satisfying appreciation has come from other filmmakers. Sometimes they have paid tribute in the form of appreciative comments. Alan Parker, the director of *Midnight Express* (1978), named among his favorite films *Raging Bull*, which he characterized as a film that was able to find an audience yet "keep the creative integrity in tact." Describing his reaction to the film the first time he saw it, Parker reflected, "When I came out of *Raging Bull*, I thought, 'I will never make a film as good as that.' And I thought, 'I might not make a film as good as that, but that's why I want to keep doing it, because maybe one day I will.'"[18]

Often the tribute other filmmakers have paid to *Raging Bull* has come in the form of allusion and homage. Perhaps no recent filmmaker has referenced Scorsese's film more than Guy Ritchie. In *Lock, Stock, and Two Smoking Barrels* (1998), Ritchie created a scene patterned on the one where Joe Pesci slams Salvy (Frank Vincent) in a taxicab door. The boxing sequences in Ritchie's follow-up film, *Snatch* (2000), echo the boxing sequences in *Raging Bull*. In addition, films that have cast Robert De Niro and Cathy Moriarty together – *Cop Land* (1997), *Analyze That* (2002) – deliberately invoke memories of *Raging Bull*. Even as we see old Cathy Moriarty, we think of young Cathy Moriarty.

The filmmakers who have alluded to *Raging Bull* include Scorsese himself. Two examples will suffice. Explaining to Jake the rationale behind matching him with Tony Janiro, Joey concludes, "If you win, you win; if you lose, you still win." In *The Color of Money* (1986), Paul Newman tells Tom Cruise that he will let him know when to win or lose because "sometimes if you lose, you win." In *Raging Bull*, Robert De Niro, as Jake La Motta, repeats the words "I'm the boss" as a kind of mantra before he goes into the ring and before he goes on stage at the Barbizon Plaza. In *Casino*, Robert De Niro, as Sam Rothstein, explains to a reporter that he is the boss of the Tangiers Casino, and his words are reprinted in a newspaper headline: "Sam Rothstein: 'I'm the Boss.'"

These self-allusions stem less from egotism on Scorsese's part than from a deliberate attempt to link his various works together into a unified body of work. At least since the time of *Raging Bull*, and perhaps earlier, Scorsese has seen his endeavor as a filmmaker as an effort to "build an oeuvre that will last" (*MSI*, 97). The verbal parallels between *Raging Bull* and his later films serve to link them together or, more precisely, serve as explicit reminders of links that are already implicit. After all, these key themes – winning, losing, being the boss – pervade Scorsese's impressive oeuvre.

Putting together a crew of scholars and a list of topics for this collection of essays, I have located contributors from different disciplines – film studies, literary history, theater history – who discuss the film from a variety of perspectives. Though primarily directed toward undergraduate and graduate film students, this collection should enhance appreciation of *Raging Bull* for all readers. I have encouraged my contributors to be as wide-ranging as possible and to situate their essays within Scorsese's oeuvre and, indeed, within the history of world cinema. Contributors to this volume have been issued a challenge: to write chapters that contain fundamental information for students, to include new information and ideas for seasoned film scholars, and to write in a jargon-free style that all readers can appreciate. Regardless of individual focus, each of the following chapters presents a combination of general overview and original insight.

In Chapter 1, "Art and Genre in *Raging Bull*," Leger Grindon follows up on Pauline Kael's suggestive description of *Raging Bull* as "a biography of the genre of prizefight films" by examining it within the context of the boxing film tradition. He identifies broad trends within the boxing genre as they bear on Scorsese's film, in particular the integration of the boxer and the gangster initiated in 1937 with *Kid Galahad*, the influence of noir stylistics in the cycle after World War II, the tradition of the boxing biopic, and the impact of films from the early 1950s about boxers after they leave the ring. Grindon also examines how *Raging Bull* reaches beyond the Hollywood tradition to embrace qualities characteristic of European art cinema.

Incorporating numerous conflicting film styles – gritty realism with graphic expressionism, Eisenstein-style montage with fluid tracking shots – *Raging Bull* sometimes approaches the brink of stylistic incoherence, but it never allows audiences to fully recognize how close it comes to an artistic fiasco. In Chapter 2, "Visual Absurdity in *Raging Bull*," Todd Berliner presents a sophisticated analysis of the film's incongruous imagery and visual styles. *Raging Bull*, Berliner argues, causes spectators to register its visual incongruities as if they were not incongruities and to make sense of combinations of images that no logical mind could reasonably understand. Because it seems coherent but is not, *Raging Bull* remains a step removed from perfect intelligibility, and efforts to understand it only make the film seem more elusive.

Drawing on contemporary performance theory, Michael Peterson argues in Chapter 3, "*Raging Bull* and the Idea of Performance," that the film uses a performance frame to comprehend Jake La Motta's life. The idea of performance also serves as an interpretive key to the film's themes, to its marketing, and to the careers of both La Motta and De Niro. *Raging Bull* juxtaposes La Motta's athletic performance as a fighter with his later cultural performances as a celebrity attraction. His athletic performance is driven by the masculine animal power suggested by the title, whereas his stand-up appearances imply a pitiable reduction and confinement of his beastly side.

As a means of exploring Jake La Motta's attitude toward women, Peggy McCormack contrasts Scorsese's depiction of Jake's subjective, paranoid, surrealistic point of view with his use of an objective viewpoint that contradicts Jake's suspicions in Chapter 4, "Women in *Raging Bull*: Scorsese's Use of Determinist, Objective, and Subjective Techniques." McCormack devotes most attention to Vickie, Jake's second wife, but she also discusses Irma, his first wife, and the anonymous women who haunt the nightclubs of Jake's later years.

In Chapter 5, "My Victims, My Melancholia: *Raging Bull* and Vincente Minelli's *The Bad and the Beautiful*," Mark Nicholls parallels Jake La Motta with Jonathan Shields, the character Kirk Douglas plays in *The Bad and the Beautiful* (1952). Both victimize the ones they need to satisfy their own desires for belonging. In *Raging Bull*, Jake secretly covets the very experience of loss, sacrifice, and punishment that Joey and Vickie endure at his hands. Jake's melancholic narrative thus contains another story, a secret history, which provides the narrative pattern central to his fantasy.

Reprints of several contemporary reviews follow Chapter 5. All of the reviews included here are new finds, meaning that they have not been reprinted since their original appearance, nor have they appeared in any previous Scorsese bibliography. These reviews provide an indication of the contemporary reception of *Raging Bull*, but they also provide ideas for further thought. Recording the fact that many members of the audience cheered as Jake up-ends his dinner table, Jay Scott presents an aspect of the film's reception that has gone neglected. Identifying one of the film's thematic subtexts as "the mysterious dynamics of memory and regret," Michael Seitz offers an idea another may wish to explore at greater length. Contemporary reviewers often lack the time and space to develop their thoughts fully, but their reviews provide numerous ideas that others may wish to develop. Like any great work of art, *Raging Bull* presents nearly endless opportunities for critical exploration.

NOTES

1. Jake La Motta, Joseph Carter, and Peter Savage, *Raging Bull* (1970; reprinted, New York: Bantam, 1980), 2, 39, 109, 112.
2. La Motta, Carter, and Savage, *Raging Bull*, 240.
3. Derek Malcolm, "The Punch in Scorsese's Ring Cycle," *Guardian*, 14 February 1981, 10.
4. Martin Scorsese, "Introduction: Interview with Martin Scorsese by Paul Schrader," in *Taxi Driver*, by Paul Schrader (London: Faber and Faber, 1990), xviii.
5. Scorsese, "Introduction: Interview with Martin Scorsese by Paul Schrader," xix.
6. Malcolm, "The Punch," 10.
7. Eleanor Ringel, "*Raging Bull* Goes the Distance in Spite of Itself," *Atlanta Constitution*, 20 February 1981, 3B.
8. Peter Ackroyd, "All the Rage," *Spectator*, 28 February 1981, 26.
9. John Coleman, "Box and Cocks," *New Statesman*, 20 February 1981, 23.
10. Desson Thomson, "Inside the Skin of a Killer: Charlize Theron Tears into Role of a Lifetime in Violent *Monster*," *Washington Post*, 9 January 2004, sec. C, p. 1.
11. Lawrence O'Toole, "Going the Distance, and Much, Much Further," *Maclean's*, 1 December 1980, 73.
12. Edgar Allan Poe, *Essay and Reviews*, ed. G. R. Thompson (New York: Library of America, 1984), 782.
13. [Augustus Baldwin Longstreet,] *Georgia Scenes, Characters Incidents, &c. in the First Half Century of the Republic* (Augusta: S. R. Sentinel, 1835), 63.
14. Amy Taubin, Review of *Raging Bull*, *Village Voice*, 2–8 August 2000, <www.villagevoice.com>.
15. David A. Cook, *Lost Illusions: American Cinema in the Shadow of Watergate and Vietnam, 1970–1979* (2000; reprinted, Berkeley: University of California Press, 2002), 212.
16. Jean-Luc Godard, *Godard on Godard*, ed. Jean Narboni, trans. Tom Milne (1972; reprinted, New York: Da Capo, 1986), 239.
17. Carlin A. Barton, "The Scandal of the Arena," *Representations* 27 (1989): 33.
18. Alastair Mckay, "Interview: Alan Parker, Director's Cut," *Scotsman*, 19 November 2003, 13.

I Art and Genre in *Raging Bull*

Genre films are based upon a shared formula, conventions that are subconsciously recognized by audiences and filmmakers. Repetitive genre patterns are often understood to be contrary to the originality, complexity, and intensity characteristic of high art. Indeed, the European "art" cinema has often been distinguished from Hollywood productions because it turns from genre conventions and presents films with a greater emphasis on social realism, the psychological development of characters, self-conscious style, and a cultivated ambiguity.

Paradoxically, many of the most celebrated cinematic achievements of Hollywood filmmaking are vividly realized genre films. Many classics of the studio era, such as *Trouble in Paradise* (1932), *The Big Sleep* (1946), and *Vertigo* (1958), were recognized as little more than generic entertainments at the time of their release. Even films from the "Hollywood Renaissance" influenced by the European art cinema, such as *2001: A Space Odyssey* (1968), *The Godfather* (1972), and *Chinatown* (1974), found their base in genre films. Noël Carroll, among others, has written of the two-tiered address of such classics – the obvious level of incident, character, and sensation engaging a mass audience, while the more subtle development of implicit themes and stylistic patterns is understood by the attentive film enthusiast.[1]

Raging Bull arises from this Hollywood tradition of using genre to construct a work that realizes ambitious aesthetic goals.[2] By contrast with *Raging Bull*, *Fat City* (1972) is a Hollywood boxing film that avoids genre conventions and builds its artistic sensibility upon its literary source. For many, the aesthetic aspiration rather than the foundation in genre was the most apparent quality in *Raging Bull*. The black-and-white cinematography, a repellent protagonist, and the ambiguous conclusion disqualified the film from being a routine entertainment. Qualities contributing to the popularity of boxing films circa 1980 – the upbeat ethos of *Rocky* (1976), the sentimentality of *The Champ* (1979), or the light-hearted humor of *The Main Event* (1979) – were conspicuous in their absence. But Pauline Kael was among those who noted the filmmaker's debt to the boxing film genre: "*Raging Bull* isn't a biographical film about a fighter's rise and fall; it's a biography of the genre of prizefight films. Scorsese loves the visual effects and the powerful melodramatic moments of movies such as *Body and Soul, The Set-Up*, and *Golden Boy*."[3] The working methods of the filmmaker testify to the influence of the boxing film genre on *Raging Bull*.

"I love movies – it's my whole life and that's it," explains Martin Scorsese (*SS*, 1). In discussing his own films, Scorsese regularly appeals to the motion pictures that have influenced him and frequently views particular movies that have bearing on his current project. Scorsese refers to, among other films, *Body and Soul* (1947), *The Quiet Man* (1952), and *On the Waterfront* (1954) as points of reference in developing *Raging Bull*.

The boxing film genre serves as a resource contributing to the artistic achievement of *Raging Bull*. I review the genre conventions governing plot, character, setting, and iconography, and I analyze how *Raging Bull* adopts and transforms these practices to achieve its artistry. An awareness of the interaction of genre conventions with cinematic art offers an illuminating perspective on *Raging Bull* – for many, including myself, the stellar achievement in the Hollywood boxing film tradition.

PLOT

Raging Bull presents a tale of the rise and fall of a boxing champion, a narrative pattern typical of the boxing film genre that goes back at least to *The Iron Man* (1931) and characterizes key works, such as

Golden Boy (1939) and *Body and Soul*, among others. By contrast, hit boxing films from the 1970s, such as *Hard Times* (1974), *Rocky*, and *The Champ*, moved away from this classic plot, though they exhibited other familiar genre traits. In addition, *Raging Bull* incorporates a flashback framework that links the film to the boxing noir movies of the 1940s, particularly *Body and Soul* and *Champion* (1949). The flashback initiates the nostalgic tone and sets the stage for the self-conscious reflection that marks the conclusion of the film, a sensibility *Raging Bull* shares with its film noir antecedents.

Numerous events characteristic of the rise-and-fall plot appear, including the rise of the fighter in a montage chronicling victorious bouts, negotiations with a gangster promoter who controls access to a title fight, and the dive required by the mob boss controlling the prizefighter. Among the noteworthy revisions in the rise and fall plot offered in *Raging Bull* is the elimination of the discovery of the boxer's talent and his early training. Instead, Scorsese jumps into La Motta's career with the middleweight already an established fighter. Rather than discovery and training episodes, the film expands the post-boxing epilogue into an elaborate "after-leaving-the-ring" segment.[4]

As with Hollywood films generally, *Raging Bull* develops a romance in parallel with the action characteristic of a particular genre. In the boxing film, the romantic couple typically posed an opposition to the male world of boxing and the predatory sensuality of the vamp. At the conclusion of the plot, the prizefighter would leave the ring to marry his sweetheart as in *Kid Galahad* (1937) or *Golden Boy*. Though there were numerous variations on the model, the motif of the beloved usually cultivated a gendered opposition between the masculine values of fighting and the feminine nurturing of romance and family. In *Raging Bull*, as in Hollywood genre films typically, the relationship between romance and a parallel action is central to the significance of the work.

An awareness of the generic plot conventions of the boxing film allows similarities and differences in *Raging Bull* to assume a meaningful perspective. The plot divides into four parts: the prelude and postscript frame that portrays Jake in his dressing room preparing his stage act; Act 1, which follows Jake's early boxing career and his courtship of Vickie, ending with the still image–home movie montage of ring victories and domestic bliss; Act 2, which portrays his quest for the middleweight title and his growing jealousy of Vickie, ending with his championship victory; and Act 3, which presents the estrangement from his brother, his loss of the title, and the end of his marriage. The key distinctions between the generic plot and *Raging Bull* are the function of boxing, the treatment of romance, the after-leaving-the-ring episodes, and the ambiguous conclusion. Each of these variations transforms a generic convention into an illuminating aesthetic device.

In discussing the plans for *Raging Bull*, Martin Scorsese declared, "One sure thing was that it wouldn't be a film about boxing! We [Scorsese and De Niro] didn't know a thing about it and it didn't interest us at all!" (*MSI*, 85). Though the film adapts the autobiography of middleweight champion Jake La Motta, the sport itself served as a means for exploring more fundamental human experience. Nevertheless, boxing in *Raging Bull* is more widely distributed and integral to the plot than is common within the Hollywood boxing genre. The boxing film generally uses the boxing sequences as important spectacles of physical action that punctuate the plot at key intervals, like the song and dance numbers in a musical. Most Hollywood boxing films display a well-established pattern of three or four boxing episodes that culminate in an extended bout at the climax of the fiction. Earlier episodes may include sparring in a gym, which results in the discovery of the boxer's talent, as in *Golden Boy*, or a montage of ring action, newspaper headlines, and speeding trains, which present the rise of a fighter on tour in, for example, *Champion*; or occasionally the protagonist will exhibit his talent in an important bout midway through the fiction and in anticipation of the concluding confrontation, as in *Hard Times*. The typical Hollywood boxing film moves steadily toward an extended bout that brings the film to its climax. As a result, we anticipate the final boxing match, like the concluding chase in the crime film or the confrontation with the monster in horror, as the culmination of the fiction.

Raging Bull changes this plotting significantly by adding more bouts. There are nine boxing sequences, counting the montage condensation as one episode, spread from the beginning of the flashback in 1941 to Jake's loss of the middleweight title about three-quarters of the way through the film. Together, they run approximately nineteen and a half minutes, about fifteen percent of the movie. Though the number and range of bouts are increased, Scorsese removes boxing from the conclusion. Rather, after Jake's retirement, various other performances, as well as his struggle in a prison cell, suggest a series of ring analogies that are related to the motifs and themes of the earlier bouts.

An expressionistic principle of interiority distinguishes these sequences. They portray the inner feelings of the boxer, rather than a spectacle concept of exhibition or exteriority designed to replicate the experience of an audience at a boxing match. I will discuss the boxing sequences with regard to setting and iconography, but at this point, note that Scorsese's plotting of the bouts functions to intensify the physical action through a wider distribution and to intensify the emotional content by basing his design, not upon the experience of the spectator, but on that of the boxer. Scorsese explains, "I wanted to do the ring scenes as if the viewers were the fighter and their impressions were the fighter's – of what he would think or feel, what he would hear" (Kelly, 132). This expressive approach facilitates continuing the motif of interiority in similar episodes after the boxer retires from the ring.

The relationship of the boxing sequences to *Raging Bull* as a whole is closer to a practice in the European art cinema than to the typical Hollywood boxing film because the subjective style of these sequences is distinct from the more objective qualities shaping the body of the film. Take a Scorsese favorite for comparison, Fellini's *8½* (1963), in which Guido's dreams, memories, and fantasies are presented in a much more lyrical, exaggerated, and symbolic manner than the social reality Guido experiences in common with the other characters. In a similar fashion, the heroine's memory in *Hiroshima, Mon Amour* (1959) is given special treatment. That is, the subjective experience of characters in the art cinema frequently receives an exceptional form that both intensifies and marks off that experience. Such a pattern offers a precedent for the boxing sequences in *Raging Bull*, but the Scorsese picture offers an experience of intense physical interaction, the exchange of blows, rather than the reverie or self-conscious reflection characteristic of "art" films. *Raging Bull* cultivates subjectivity in the boxing episodes, but a subjectivity characterized by sensation rather than reflection. Instead of developing a text on the model of dream imagery and association, the boxing sequences strive for a more physiological reaction to stimuli closer to Sergei Eisenstein's behaviorialist concepts of a montage that aimed to "plow the psyche" of the spectator (Figure 4).

Romance in *Raging Bull* parallels the rise and fall of La Motta's ring career. The relationship between Jake and Vickie avoids the simple counterpoint between fighting and loving common to the boxing film, but rather weaves a complex interaction between La Motta's relationship to his wife and his ring exploits. Scorsese ends Act 1 with the couple marrying, rather than using the romantic union at the conclusion to usher the boxer from the ring. The champion's fall extends beyond the loss of his title to include separation from the beloved. Most important is the displacement the plotting develops between boxing and romance. The first lovemaking encounters between Jake and Vickie are arranged between the bouts with Sugar Ray Robinson. In the first, a photo of Jake and Joey in playful fisticuffs holds the screen as Jake and Vickie move off toward the bed and then the film cuts to the Robinson bout. The next episode finds Jake dousing his genitals with ice water to interrupt foreplay with Vickie because he does not want sex to weaken his fighting power. The Robinson bout immediately follows. After the decision for Robinson, Jake soaks his bruised hand in ice water, echoing the earlier gesture and suggesting a parallel between his physical embrace of Vickie and his assault on his ring opponent.[5]

The most important displacement occurs in the parallel between Jake's jealousy of Vickie and his quest for the title. Jake's quest is thwarted because the gangster promoter, Tommy Como, who oversees boxing, will not give the contender a title shot unless he takes a dive on instructions from the mob. In spite of his determination to win the title on his own merits, Jake has to relent and takes the fall against Jimmy Fox. Jake's powerlessness to control his destiny, in spite of his domination in the ring, results in impotence and jealousy. Weaving together domestic scenes and prizefighting, the movie portrays the boxer projecting his guilt at having to compromise his skills onto his innocent wife. His marriage is infected with the corruption of prizefighting. The association is underlined in the scene where

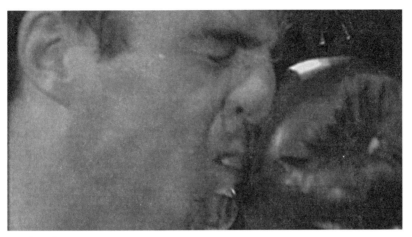

4. Kino-fist.

Joey reports to Jake on his meeting with Como. The brothers meet at the neighborhood swimming pool where Jake was introduced to Vickie. However, a summer rainstorm falls as Joey breaks the news that the boxer must take the dive. The pool is associated with romance, but the storm darkens the link. Before hearing Joey's report, Jake begins to rant against Vickie's infidelity. Controlling his anger at the mob, La Motta redirects his rage at his wife. Jealousy of other boxers, and even of the aged Como, amplifies the relationship between romance and boxing in Jake's tormented consciousness. Rather than portraying the idealization of courtship common to the boxing film genre, *Raging Bull* presents self-destructive, neurotic conjugal sexuality as central to the couple. As a result of interweaving the romance and boxing, the plot of *Raging Bull* suggests a complex psychological relationship that builds upon a generic convention but elaborates it in a fresh and illuminating manner.

Most boxing films conclude with the prizefighter ending his ring career after the climactic bout. Usually a brief post-boxing episode ties up the film, such as the death of the boxer in *Champion* or the victory parade in *Somebody Up There Likes Me* (1956). However, I have argued that there are a series of important films from the early 1950s that take the generic boxing plot as a backstory and develop the film around the boxer's experience after leaving the ring. These films include

The Quiet Man, From Here to Eternity (1953), and *On the Waterfront*. *Raging Bull* displays the influence of these films. Martin Scorsese has explicitly cited *The Quiet Man* and *On the Waterfront* among his points of reference, and he develops La Motta's story after his retirement from 1956 to 1964 in a series of episodes that constitute the conclusion of the film.

Four actions during these episodes evoke the interiority that characterizes the boxing sequences. Two are stand-up stage routines, the first in La Motta's Miami club and the second in a sleazy Manhattan lounge. A third finds Jake incarcerated in the Dade County Stockade where he pounds the wall and mutters to himself. The final episode portrays the performer alone in his dressing room reciting his lines to a mirror. All four suggest a similarity with the earlier boxing episodes by placing Jake on a stage or other enclosed, isolated space, by alluding to boxing, and by portraying Jake's interior struggles.

After-leaving-the-ring films send their protagonist on a quest for value. The experience of boxing is primarily physical, and the close of the ring career brings with it a crisis. The boxer, who achieved his self-esteem through his fighting prowess, must find value apart from the physical. In *The Quiet Man*, Sean Thornton seeks his ethnic roots in Ireland, strives to overcome his guilt at killing a man in the ring, and weds Mary Kate to begin a new life. Prewitt in *From Here to Eternity* seeks fellowship in the army and love from Alma. Terry Malloy in *On the Waterfront* wants to clear his conscience and gain self-respect after betraying his skills in the ring and conspiring in the murder of his friend.

Scorsese never completely accounts for Jake La Motta's rage nor absolves his brutality. But the post-boxing episodes calm his protagonist as he moves toward reflection and self-examination. Jake's retirement is introduced with an interview. The former boxer appears with his wife and children at the poolside of his Florida home. Family, home, and prosperity serve as the standard culmination of the boxing film, the successful romance bringing domestic contentment. However, Jake's grotesque, fat body belies his declared satisfaction. The following scenes at his club set up his next fall.

The stand-up comic routine Jake offers his club patrons explicitly evokes his boxing. The introductory music plays the "Gillette Blue

Blades" theme, evoking television boxing. His closing verse compares his comic performance to boxing Sugar Ray, concluding:

> So gimme a stage
> Where this bull here can rage
> And though I can fight
> I'd much rather hear myself recite.
> That's entertainment.

The performance also mixes boxing with Jake's marriage. He announces to his audience that he is about to celebrate his eleventh wedding anniversary and then tells a joke that mocks marriage, with the suggestion that a husband offers his wife to a friend. Indeed, before the Miami club sequence ends, Jake is presented in sexually compromising behavior and Vickie shows up to announce that she is divorcing him. The image of retirement bliss shatters. Jake's club is another ring in which he plays out emotions without understanding or contrition.

Jake's fall reaches its nadir when he is thrown into the Dade County Stockade. Again, the scene mixes interiority and boxing but adds a note of reflection. Locked into a shadowy, confining cell Jake begins pounding first his head, then his fists and arms against the concrete wall, shouting to himself "Why, why, why?" and repeatedly weeping "You're so stupid.... I'm not an animal." Here, the brute finally chides himself and inflicts the punishment previously administered by his boxing opponents. While he is still in the cell, voice-over sound bridges forward to Jake in another stand-up routine at the sleazy Hotel Markwell in Manhattan the following year. Responding to hecklers in the small audience, the comic threatens to make a "comeback." His contentious repartee again links his ring battles and his stage performances. However, rather than brawling, Jake tries to make peace. After leaving the club, he bumps into his brother Joey on the street and makes an awkward attempt at reconciliation. The self-realization in prison has softened the former boxer, even though his brother greets Jake's gesture with wary reserve. La Motta has moved beyond his raging sensations to reflection and toward retribution.

The closing scene returns to the framing episode where the film began. The flashback suggests memory without explicitly having Jake recall his past. The audience observes the boxer's history but remains uncertain as to whether Jake is pondering it himself. The boxing noir films *Body and Soul* and *Champion* also employed a flashback frame to cultivate reflection in the boxer, but then returned to the present before the big fight brought the film to a close. But for *Raging Bull*, the move from sensation to reflection is the conclusion.

The final dressing room scene suggests interiority through setting and allusion without letting the protagonist acknowledge his thoughts or express understanding. The scene finds La Motta alone facing a mirror. However, the pose of self-examination is qualified because Jake is practicing his stage routine. Scorsese uses a reference to the boxing film genre to bring his film to a close. La Motta recites Terry Malloy's famous speech to his brother Charlie in a taxicab from *On the Waterfront*. Here, Terry blames his brother for sabotaging his boxing career by making him take a dive for racketeers. The allusion uses the genre as a source for a penetrating complexity.

The director reports that Robert De Niro performed nineteen takes and that take thirteen was used – a performance in which the speech is given with little inflection or dramatic color. Scorsese claimed that the only way to deliver it was "so cold that you concentrate on the words" (*SS*, 77). It opens with "Charlie, it was you" and closes with Jake repeating twice "It was you, Charlie." With La Motta looking in the mirror as he speaks, an ambiguity arises. That is, does "Charlie" refer to Jake's brother Joey, who seems to be in an analogous situation with Terry's brother Charlie, or does Jake staring at himself in the mirror imply that he himself is culpable? Does Jake blame his brother for his compromises, his ring failures, Vickie's ostensible infidelities? Or has he finally faced up to his own responsibility? "When he says in the mirror, 'It was you, Charlie,' is he playing his brother, or putting the blame on himself? It's certainly very disturbing for me," Scorsese acknowledges (*SS*, 77). Scorsese's incorporation of the film reference allows the ambiguity to simmer. De Niro's cool, detached delivery and his blank response give no clue.

After his rehearsal, a voice calls from offscreen telling the "Champ" he is on in five minutes. Before facing his audience, Jake rises, says to the mirror, "Go get'em Champ," assumes a boxer's pose, and lets loose with a flurry of warm-up punches while repeatedly muttering, "I'm the boss." The analogy between the dressing room and boxing is underlined as the film ends. Both have served as arenas for Jake's inner struggle. In the prison cell, Jake expresses introspection and regret, and he appeals to his humanity. But in the dressing room, the boxer's understanding of his fall remains ambiguous, qualified at best.

La Motta has been moving from sensation to reflection just as he has gone from being a fighter to becoming a stage performer. Before the camera enters the dressing room, a sign invites the public to see Jake La Motta performing the words of Shakespeare and Tennessee Williams, among others. The after-leaving-the-ring episodes call up the art motif in the boxing film genre. From Joe Bonaparte's violin in *Golden Boy*, to Prewitt's trumpet in *From Here to Eternity* and Rocky running up the steps of the Philadelphia Art Museum, art holds its place in the genre, generally as an alternative to boxing. In *Raging Bull*, the move to art serves as the avenue to reflection and as a meaningful turn from the blinding sensation of the boxing ring.

Jake's recitation from *On the Waterfront* prepares for the literary passage that closes the film. Scorsese presents with deliberation a quotation from John's gospel as part of a dedication to his recently deceased film teacher, Haig P. Manoogian. In the passage, the Pharisees identify a "fellow" [Jesus] known to be a "sinner" to a man whose sight was restored by Christ. The man replies, "Whether or not he was a sinner, I do not know. . . . All I know is this: once I was blind and now I can see." The Biblical text points in two directions. Most obviously, the student is saluting his mentor for shaping his vision as a filmmaker. On the other hand, the sinner evokes Jake La Motta, the wild brute who arose out of New York's Italian-American ghetto when young Scorsese was growing up. In interviews, the director claims that his engagement in the work arose from his similarities with La Motta. Furthermore, the filmmaker acknowledges that the production was initiated when he was coming out of a deep personal crisis. As a result, the passage from John suggests that the boxer's anguish has given Scorsese perspective on his own raging spirit. The filmmaker has found in the cinema a means of reflecting upon the Italian-American culture from which he arose. He has used that instrument, his art, as a means of gaining insight that he hopes to pass along to his audience.

CHARACTERS

The character types populating the boxing film genre are recogniz-
ably at play in *Raging Bull*, but they have been given a fresh, more
complex humanity. Tommy Como is the gangster promoter controlling the boxing racket. The stock figure is recognizable in the genre
as early as Humphrey Bogart's Turkey Morgan in *Kid Galahad*, fully
developed with Eddie Fuseli in *Golden Boy*, and realized most mem-
orably in Roberts from *Body and Soul*. However, Tommy Como acts
more like a wise grandfather than a criminal operator using intimida-
tion and violence to impose his authority. He is older and softer than
the gangster overlord in La Motta's autobiography. Tommy courts
the boxer with drinks and flattery, serves as a peacemaker between
Joey and Salvy, and negotiates with Joey, offering rewards in return
for cooperation. Compared with the swaggering belligerence of Jake,
Tommy Como acts like a neighborhood elder. Because La Motta's
chief antagonist is patient and affable, the boxer seems even more
stubborn in his refusal to come to terms. *Raging Bull* dissolves a simplistic opposition between the integrity of an athlete and a greedy
racketeer but conjures up generic figures to help the audience understand the characters from a new perspective.

Joey La Motta is another illuminating case. The boxer's brother is
a long-standing character usually employed to express qualities in
contrast to the boxer. In *City for Conquest* (1940), the brother is a
talented musician whose education the boxer finances with prizefighting. In *Champion*, the brother is a crippled saint scolding Midge
Kelly's demonic roughneck; in *Rocky*, Paulie, Balboa's brother-in-law-
to-be, serves to underline the boxer's innocence with his bitterness.
Raging Bull combines two characters from the autobiography, Joey La
Motta and Pete Savage, the boxer's close friend, into the more generic
screen brother. Rather than illuminating the protagonist through
opposition, Joey shares a perverse Italian-American machismo with
Jake. Similar in personality but less extreme than his brother, Joey
La Motta emphasizes that their behavior is a product of a widespread
ethos, not simply the malaise of a crazy boxer. When Joey finds Vickie
at the Copacabana sharing drinks with Salvy, his furious attack on
Salvy mirrors what Jake might have done. Later, when Jake storms
over to Joey's home to assault his brother, the camera anticipates

Jake's attack, showing Joey threatening to stab his child at the dinner table if the boy puts his hand on his plate one more time. The violence that constantly spills out of the boxing ring and into daily life gains credibility from Joey, who stands apart from the exceptional physicality embodied by the boxer. *Raging Bull* appeals to realism by resisting a melodramatic polarity between stock figures. Instead, it gains conviction by going against generic expectations.

The most striking aspect of character in *Raging Bull* is its repellent protagonist. As Cis Corman, the casting director, observed after reading the script, "Jake La Motta is a terrible, evil man. Why would you want to do a movie about this?" (Kelly, 128). Most mainstream films engage the audience through their sympathy for its characters. The boxing film genre underlines this sympathy with the habits of spectator sports, rooting for the competitor who has gained our familiarity. La Motta's thuggish self-indulgence accented by his abusive treatment of women, his racism, and his semi-literate, obscene language must make him one of the most repellent protagonists in motion picture history. The initial press response to the film respected its craft but was disquieted by its brutal subject. *Raging Bull* allies the audience forcefully to Jake; he appears in nearly every scene, and his behavior is the foundation for the dramatic action. How is the viewer to cope with what becomes an assault on humane sensibilities?

Jake La Motta is not the first anti-hero in the boxing film. Midge Kelly, the protagonist of *Champion*, was also a rogue, as was his literary model in Ring Lardner's short story. But *Champion* spent most of its resources explaining how Midge became a heartless bully, and our sympathy was enlisted as he fought back against exploitation, only to become an exploiter himself. Furthermore, he was punished with estrangement, suffering, and death – not to mention the condemnation of the righteous. The constraints of studio-era censorship softened Kelly's sins in comparison with the outrageous behavior in *Raging Bull*. The psychological explanation of Kelly's motivation complemented by the moral condemnation of his mistreatment of others softened the impact of this rogue hero. *Raging Bull* refuses both of these options.

In numerous interviews, Martin Scorsese has dismissed the simplistic psychology found in Jake La Motta's autobiography. "Jake is constantly analyzing himself in the book. He very pedantically explains why he did this or that. But I didn't think that Jake was really able to analyze himself like that" (*MSI*, 85). *Raging Bull* avoids portraying a psychological explanation for its protagonist. In this regard, it stands in sharp contrast to *Somebody Up There Likes Me* or *Champion*.

Somebody Up There Likes Me is another film adaptation of the autobiography of a middleweight champion, Rocky Graziano. Graziano offers striking similarities to La Motta. In fact, as young toughs, they terrorized New York's Lower East Side together. Both went to prison, where they developed their roughneck skills to become successful prizefighters after their release. Each of them became the middleweight champion for a brief time. After leaving the ring, Graziano had a successful TV career, and he helped Jake La Motta get his start in show business. *Somebody Up There Likes Me* was a hit film directed by Robert Wise, from a screenplay by Ernest Lehman, that helped propel Paul Newman to stardom. In the film, Rocky's juvenile delinquency is the result of an abusive, drunken father, urban poverty, and a lack of nurturing. However, with the help of a prison chaplain, a paternal manager, and a loving, tender wife, Rocky pulls his life together. He uses boxing to purge his anger at childhood mistreatment and becomes a lovable everyman. Before the title bout, Graziano has a confrontation with his father that lays his psychic anxieties to rest and allows him to realize his championship dream. The film ends in a celebratory victory parade. Scorsese criticizes La Motta's book because "the book's psychology is close to that of the 50s" (*MSI*, 86). *Somebody Up There Likes Me* illustrates what the director sought to avoid. Even though the autobiography portrays La Motta's early years in detail, Scorsese refuses to indulge in a psychological history as a means of explaining the boxer's behavior.

Talking about *Raging Bull*, Martin Scorsese explained, "The motive became to achieve an understanding of a self-destructive lifestyle" (Kelly, 122). However, it is important to note that self-understanding eludes Jake, though he quiets his rage. Scorsese and Robert De Niro build La Motta's character in *Raging Bull* on a combination of perverse realism and a disturbing subjectivity ultimately directed at audience understanding through a mix of immersion and detachment.

Realism in the arts has long been attracted to the common and the ugly as a means of undermining the idealization of form closely allied to aesthetic value. Realism made truth paramount over beauty and precise attention to social detail more important than the classical harmony of genre. The realism of *Raging Bull* strives for authentic social detail that cultivates the repellent and perverse. For example, the fights were carefully modeled on films and written records of the actual contests, and Jake La Motta coached De Niro's ring craft, but their exaggerated brutality and bloodshed make the audience wince in horror. A highly publicized aspect of realism in *Raging Bull* was Robert De Niro's enormous weight gain to play the late episodes. For the actor to shed his trim fighting physique, the production shut down filming for months while the star ate his way through France and Italy. The public was amazed that the actor had disfigured his body to such an extent. Scorsese remembers that De Niro's weight was so extreme that his breathing became labored and he lacked the stamina to do many takes. The actor explains, "As far as my gaining the weight, the external speaks for itself. But the internal changes, how you feel and how it makes you behave – for me to play the character it was the best thing I could have done. Just by having the weight on, it really made me feel a certain way, and behave a certain way" (Kelly, 143).

In addition, common period details set the stage for the dramatic action and often contrasted the mundane with the outrageous. For example, the faulty reception of a 1950 television set prompts the quarrel that tears the brothers apart. "We came up with the scene right on the set," De Niro recalls. "We said, 'How about fixing a TV?' Some stupid, little, domestic sort of thing, where there's an incident waiting to happen. It can erupt from the most mundane kind of thing that just triggers something off and then that's it. . . . all of a sudden it creates a drama" (Kelly, 140). The prop serves as an analogue for the breakdown in communication between Jake and Joey. These precise details anchor the incident in a specific time and place, even as Jake's outlandish accusation of adultery gives the episode a perverse, almost unbelievable, sense of human folly.

Film noir of the 1940s, preeminently *Double Indemnity* (1944), brought a fresh perspective to the psychology of the crime film by presenting the drama from the perspective of the criminal. The audience becomes closer to the crime itself and shares in the lure of the forbidden. The indulgence in outlaw behavior carries with it a fascination, even as the emotional alliance leads the audience, along with the characters, to doom. *Raging Bull* borrows from this noir perspective by allying the viewer so closely to Jake's twisted subjectivity. As De Niro noted, "Jake himself is primitive, he can't hide certain feelings" (Kelly, 126). Jake's unrestrained aggression carries with it a forceful, but disturbing, attraction. Being with Jake in the boxing ring as he punches, bobs, and endures blows carries with it an exhilarating sensation. But gradually, Jake's loutish impositions, his demented jealousy, and eventually his assaults on his family and finally himself leave one repelled, even shaken. Finally, a detached sense of fear and awe, maybe the purging Aristotle refers to as catharsis, arises in response to Robert De Niro's boxer.

Raging Bull's Jake La Motta arose in the wake of Rocky Balboa, the Italian Stallion. The enormous commercial and critical success of *Rocky* and then *Rocky II* (1979) created a benchmark for the boxing film. *Rocky* portrays the boxer as an innocent whose simple but earnest sensibility fosters his personal triumph. He harks back to Frank Capra's movie heroes from the 1930s, Mr. Deeds and Mr. Smith. *Rocky's* pure-of-heart underdog invites an embrace. Scorsese's boxer shares Balboa's animal nature, but turns its associations upside down. As with so many other genre conventions, Scorsese takes the dominant trend and transforms its meaning. *Raging Bull* portrays La Motta as a beast whose underdeveloped humanity scars everyone he touches, even himself. Furthermore, it binds us to the boxer in spite of his repellent behavior. For Scorsese, Jake's cruelty, ignorance, and rage cannot be accounted for by child rearing, poverty, or the common explanations sought to understand human suffering. Finally, ambiguity settles over the desire to explain, and an unsatisfying recognition of limitations takes hold, a need to face the mysterious complexity of human behavior. To experience compassion for this man takes the viewer to a strange and complicated feeling. The push and pull of immersion and detachment, sensation, and reflection leave you exhausted, but the experience asks you to take stock of a fresh understanding that fulfills the promise of art striving to realize its highest aspirations.

SETTING AND ICONOGRAPHY

Central to the iconography of the boxing film is the relationship between boxing and life independent of the ring. *Raging Bull* addresses
this distinction with complexity and insight. The film differentiates
and weaves together a realistic treatment of the historical era and the
subjectivity of the boxer, Jake La Motta. A stylistic distinction divides
the scenes of social interaction from the subjectivity of the boxing
episodes. For scenes of personal exchange, Scorsese employs a simple camera style favoring classic shot–counter shot or long takes that
encourages improvisation in performance. The boxing sequences, on
the other hand, were meticulously designed with storyboards, greater
camera movement, closer perspectives, and faster cutting for a much
more precise treatment of gesture and movement. The sound design
was also distinctive, with the dramatic scenes using standard recording, whereas the boxing scenes were fortified with Dolby stereo. As
a result, the distinction between social life and boxing was sharply
drawn, only to have the division evolve into a fundamental connection during the after-leaving-the-ring episodes, when the evocation
of boxing merges subjectivity with the style portraying everyday life.
As a result, the setting and iconography developed the relationship
between the Italian-American culture and the false consciousness it
cultivated – the rule-bound violence of prizefighting and the un-
fettered brutality that spilled into daily life, the conventions of the
boxing genre and the self-conscious style of an art film.

In trying to make a case to his backers for a black-and-white *Raging
Bull*, Scorsese described a period look based on documentary style. "I
want it to be something very special. On top of that, though, it would
also help us with the period look of the film," Scorsese told them "We
had an idea of making the film look like a tabloid, like the *Daily News*,
like Weegee photographs" (Kelly, 125). As a result, Scorsese often designed shots based on newspaper or magazine photos reporting on
events in the film, such as Jake kissing the canvas with his gloves
after his victory over Dauthuile and Vickie crying with her face in
her hands during the third Robinson bout. The iconography of the
popular press calls up ethnic New York in the 1940s and 50s and
adds to the historical tone of the biography film. Martin Scorsese's

experience as a documentary filmmaker helped him to fashion a realistic treatment of his nonfiction subject. Indeed, many boxing films in the past, such as *Golden Boy* or, most conspicuously, *The Joe Louis Story* (1953), incorporated newsreel footage along with staged scenes. *Raging Bull* employs a variety of documentary elements to underscore its authenticity, including titles announcing the year, city, and opponents in the bouts, the actual radio announcer's ringside description of the Dauthuile fight, and footage from the television broadcast of the Robinson championship bout. *Raging Bull* develops the tradition of urban realism in the boxing film often associated with ethnic New York. In doing so, the film re-creates the Italian-American culture that produced La Motta and shaped the young Scorsese. The film's iconography cultivates the intersection between the boxer and the filmmaker as products of ethnic New York.

The director enhances the intersection between realism and subjectivity by using objects, settings, and episodes from his own experience as an Italian-American growing up in New York City in the 1940s and 1950s. Scorsese's father plays a member of Tommy Como's entourage. The crucifix over Jake and Vickie's marriage bed was taken from Scorsese's parents' bedroom, and the Italian landscape picture hanging over the kitchen table where Jake and Vickie flirt on their first date is from Scorsese's grandmother's apartment on Elizabeth Street. The church dance was filmed in the location where Scorsese's parish held dances when he was growing up. Scorsese modeled the quarrel between Jake and his first wife on childhood memories of fights between his parents.[6] The improvisation encouraged by the director frequently intertwines the experience of La Motta and Scorsese. For example, Joey's wedding party on the roof was modeled after the wedding party of Scorsese's parents. When Marty got sick during production, Papa Scorsese was told by his son to "Go up there and direct it." As a result, the buffet was changed, candelabras were taken away, and the players were encouraged to behave as the filmmaker's father remembered the party (Kelly, 137–138). The scene itself was shot like a home movie, further embellishing the documentary tone. As a result, the realistic treatment of ethnic New York intertwines the memories and associations of the filmmaker's Italian-American experience with that of Jake La Motta. Of course, the career of the champion itself played a part in the Italian-American culture of Martin Scorsese's youth. As a result, the careful reconstruction of historical detail develops alongside the filmmaker's own emotionally charged associations.

Boxing is central to the fight film, and *Raging Bull* portrays its ring battles with a distinctive iconography based on subjectivity and sensation. The boxing matches in Hollywood feature films typically replicate the experience of the fan at ringside. *Raging Bull* turns from the optimal view of a spectator to the experience of the boxer in the ring. *Raging Bull* employs an array of image and sound devices to portray Jake La Motta's emotions in the course of the fight. Most noteworthy is that the camera almost always stays in the ring with Jake rather than shooting from the side or above the ring. The film develops the sense that inside the ring becomes equivalent to inside Jake's psyche. Earlier boxing films, such as *Kid Galahad*, *Body and Soul*, and *Somebody Up There Likes Me*, have shots within the ring that intercut with more distant perspectives and highlight the decisive moments of the bout; but no boxing film has designed its fighting sequences almost exclusively within the ring and employed that distinctive view as a basis for the boxer's subjectivity. To realize this design, Scorsese employed storyboarding, a production technique used only for these sequences. The tight shots amplify the impact of swift camera movements and quick cuts on action to convey the intensity of the fight. As a result, the camera presents hitting and being hit with a sensational immediacy.

One influential model for the design of the boxing sequences that Scorsese has acknowledged is a brief episode (67 seconds) in John Ford's *The Quiet Man*. Here, the protagonist remembers, in a highly subjective fashion distinct in style from the balance of the film, an experience in the ring. The protagonist's vision arises from a blow he receives at a wedding party, and his grief-stricken stare frames the memory. However, there is no boxing: rather, from within the ring, the camera shoots reactions to the death of a fighter after a fatal knockout. *The Quiet Man* presents the episode in the manner of a silent film: only music accented with a little background noise breaks the quiet. The characters, presented in a montage, pose, strongly foregrounded and almost still, except for a telling gesture, such as the trainer chewing his tobacco, the doctor placing a towel over the face of the dead, or the photographers clicking their flash cameras. An intensification of subjectivity and sensation circulating around guilt and impotence links Ford's dream-like treatment and *Raging Bull*; but the episode from *The Quiet Man* constitutes an isolated minute rather than serving as the basis for a pattern of events throughout the film, as is the case with the boxing in *Raging Bull*. This intensified, expanded treatment of subjectivity moves the Scorsese production from the classic conventions of the boxing film genre toward the art film.

This subjective perspective in the Scorsese film establishes the ground on which a variety of visual devices distort and exaggerate the contest to express La Motta's emotions. For example, when Robinson or Janiro is knocked down, the falling fighter goes into slow motion, amplifying Jake's feeling of domination over his opponent. Or, how the second Robinson fight is shot with a flame before the lens to give a rippling, hazy, mirage-like quality to the image, expressing Jake's illusion of dominance before he finds the judges' decision going against him (Figure 5). The exaggeration of sound effects is even more emphatically subjective than the images. Each blow in the fight is given a colorful and kinetic aural texture by the sound effects specialist Frank Warner, who has never revealed the actual sounds he manipulated. One hears a mix of amplified and distorted noises like melons cracking for punches, rifle shots for snapping flash cameras, gushing water as blood bursts from cuts, drum beats for body blows, all mixed with the rhythm and tempo of a musical score. These noises are integrated with selected natural sounds, such as shouts from the crowd, ringing bells, or an announcer's commentary. In two instances, the musical score, excerpts from the operas of Pietro Mascagni (*Cavalleria Rusticana, Guglielmo Ratcliff,* and *Silvano*), add a lyric note to the flow of noise and speech. A number of key moments, such as the knockout punch on Janiro, or the preface to Robinson's final attack on La Motta, are accented by completely eliminating this barrage of sound to produce an ominous silence. The result is an aural assault that is very different from attending a boxing match, an aesthetic experience based on distortion and exaggeration to convey the subjectivity and sensations of the fighter himself rather than the sports fan.

The association of subjectivity with ring battles sets the context for violence moving into daily life. After losing the first bout in the film

5. Third fight sequence: Fog in the frame and flames placed in front of the lens give an impression of heat.

against Jimmy Reeves, Jake's protest against the decision provokes the crowd to riot. His anger passes outside the ring to the spectators. This outburst anticipates Joey's attack on Salvy and Jake's assault on Joey and Vickie. The distinction between the ring and the social world breaks down as violence erupts in daily life. The emotional intensification of boxing links sensation and attack, so when Jake's feeling becomes unhinged outside the ring, he resorts to a physical rampage. In the closing after-leaving-the-ring episodes, the merging with daily life of the performance analogues to boxing indicate the calming of Jake's psyche as he moves from the sensations of the ring toward self-examination.

In revising the screenplay drafts of Mardik Martin and Paul Schrader, Robert De Niro and Martin Scorsese decided to have Jake recite Terry Malloy's monologue at the close because *"On the Waterfront* was our iconography" (*SS*, 77). On the one hand, the quotation from a benchmark 1954 film about an ex-boxer in ethnic New York combines period, genre, and realism that establish the context for *Raging Bull*. On the other hand, the words of Terry Malloy represent Jake's consciousness as arising from popular culture. His effort to understand himself is filtered through that culture to the point that his reflection slides into ambiguity. The boundary between that culture and the boxer's personality becomes murky. It is part of the ideology that produced Jake La Motta and Martin Scorsese; it may also become a means toward their salvation. For the audience as well as the filmmaker, genre serves as a foundation for art that guides our understanding and also bears witness to the conditions that produced it. The conventions of the boxing film genre provide *Raging Bull* with the correlates for a penetrating artistic vision.

NOTES

1. Noël Carroll, *Interpreting the Moving Image* (New York: Cambridge University Press, 1998), 240–264.
2. For another treatment of *Raging Bull* that addresses genre among other issues, see Frank P. Tomasulo, "Raging Bully: Postmodern Violence and Masculinity in *Raging Bull*," *Mythologies of Violence in Postmodern Media*, ed. Christopher Sharrett (Detroit: Wayne State University Press, 1999), 175–197.
3. Pauline Kael, "The Current Cinema: Religious Pulp, or the Incredible Hulk," *New Yorker*, 8 December 1980, 217. Colin L. Westerbeck, Jr., makes a similar observation in "Shadowboxing: A Fighter's Stance Toward Life," *Commonweal*, 16 January 1981, 20.
4. Leger Grindon, "The Structure of Meaning in the Boxing Film Genre," *Cinema Journal* 35, no. 4 (1996): 54–69.
5. Robin Wood, *Hollywood from Vietnam to Reagan* (New York: Columbia University Press, 1986), 245–269, notes this association and argues that it signifies a repressed homosexual desire Jake experiences for his ring opponents.
6. Martin Scorsese and Thelma Schoonmaker, audio commentary, *Raging Bull* (Santa Monica: Criterion, 1990).

2 Visual Absurdity in *Raging Bull*

Visually, *Raging Bull* is almost an artistic fiasco. The film's visual style seems often on the point of falling to pieces. The last fight scene, for instance – in which Sugar Ray Robinson incessantly pummels an exhausted Jake La Motta – depicts images so ludicrous that it's a wonder that viewers can make sense of it. One shot bizarrely shows a punch from the perspective of Robinson's glove as it approaches La Motta's face. Seconds later, one of Robinson's blows causes liquid to spray out of La Motta's head, as though from a sprinkler, and splatter a crowd of onlookers with what looks like a bucket-load of blood. At one point Robinson winds up for a punch in a ridiculously awkward stance, his arm and shoulder stretched in the air behind him, standing like a third-grader pretending to be a fighter: The shot appears more strange because of slow-motion cinematography and the curious emergence of smoke surrounding Robinson's body. Such absurd and implausible images permeate the film, especially its fight sequences.

In the pages that follow, I shall set about demonstrating that *Raging Bull*'s visual incoherence and intermittent absurdity are integral to its success as a film and one of the primary reasons that critics and audiences find the film so compelling. Before I do, however, I want to illustrate director Martin Scorsese's commitment to the film by discussing the care with which he constructed its eccentric visual style.

"I put everything I knew and felt into that film and I thought it would be the end of my career," Scorsese said. "It was what I call a kamikaze way of making movies: pour everything in, then forget all about it and go find another way of life" (*SS*, 77). To prepare the eight elaborate fight sequences, Scorsese and director of photography Michael Chapman mapped out every camera angle, camera movement, and distance of framing, as well as every actor's movement and every punch. Chapman said, "Each shot was drawn out in great detail, almost like Arthur Murray, those weird dance steps they used to draw on the floor. We did that" (Kelly, 132). Together, the fight scenes last about nineteen minutes of screen time in the 129-minute movie, but they took ten weeks to shoot in a film that shot for a total of sixteen weeks.

Scorsese and Chapman filmed each fight sequence in a different style. For instance, image-distorting techniques during the third fight (between La Motta and Sugar Ray Robinson) convey an impression of heat throughout: A heavy haze fills most of the frames, figures come in and out of focus, long lenses and slow-motion cinematography make the movements of the characters look sluggish, and several shots display a desert-mirage effect, created by putting flames in front of the lens during shooting (Figure 5). The sixth fight, which focuses on La Motta's eagerness to win Marcel Cerdon's middle-weight crown, leaves a completely different impression: This sequence has a more lyrical presentation – it's the only fight sequence with operatic background music and without an announcer's commentary – and the quick depictions of the passing rounds make La Motta's victory seem swift and assured. By contrast, the last fight sequence, in which La Motta loses the crown, focuses on the punishment he receives during the bout and seems to go on interminably: Slow-motion shots frame the blood and sweat falling off of La Motta's face; at times, the action stops and all sounds drop out, except for the sound of the boxer's panting breath, and for half a minute, discordant images of Robinson's ceaseless punching flash across the screen.

Post-production took six months (rather than the allotted seven weeks). According to editor Thelma Schoonmaker, producer Irwin Winkler said to her and Scorsese, "'You can't mix this film *inch by inch*.' And Marty said, 'That's the way it's going to be done.' And it *was*" (Kelly, 148). Her first major narrative film, *Raging Bull* won Schoonmaker an Oscar for editing. She has attributed the victory to

Scorsese's pre-production planning and the director's own editing talents: "I felt that *my* award was *his* because I know that I won it for the fight sequences, and the fight sequences are as brilliant as they are because of the way Marty thought them out. I helped him put it together, but it was not my editing skill that made that film look so good" (Kelly, 150).

The diligence Scorsese used to construct every moment of *Raging Bull* and the critical recognition the film has received, especially for its astonishing fight sequences, prompts this essay's painstakingly close examination of the film's visual style. To understand what it is about the visual style of *Raging Bull* that has earned it such recognition, one needs to consider the film, as Scorsese did when he constructed it, "inch by inch."

Raging Bull was grueling to plan, shoot, and edit, partly because it violates the logic of Hollywood's filming and editing conventions which offer filmmakers a ready-made, time-tested blueprint for keeping spatial relations coherent, for comfortably orienting spectators, and for maintaining a consistent flow of narrative information. As Hitchcock was fond of observing, however, "Nothing in the world is as dull as logic."[1] *Raging Bull* offers an aesthetically exciting alternative to Hollywood's narrative efficiency and visual coherence.[2] It rejects many of the stylistic harmonies associated with Hollywood cinema, even though it also relies on, and feels stabilized by, some traditional Hollywood structures (such as classical conventions of narration, continuity, and realism) that prevent the film from collapsing into chaos and arch unpredictability. The constant tugging activity between the film's stylistic perversities (elements that pull the film in disparate directions) and stylistic unities (elements that draw together its incongruent pieces) creates myriad potentials for disorder that the film continually checks through visual means.

To understand the kinds of incoherences that characterize *Raging Bull*'s visual style, let us first look at the ways in which the film adopts two antithetical techniques for combining images – Eisensteinian visual collisions and fluid visual transformations. Scorsese himself testified to that tension in his work when he said, "I'm torn between admiring things done in one shot, like Ophuls or Renoir, on the one hand, and the cutting of, say, Hitchcock and Eisenstein on the other."[3] Afterward, we shall see how *Raging Bull* enables spectators to register the film's various incoherences as if they were not incoherences and to understand combinations of images that no mind could reasonably understand.

RAGING BULL AND "INTELLECTUAL MONTAGE"

Interspersed throughout *Raging Bull*, Scorsese uses a type of editing espoused by Soviet filmmaker Sergei Eisenstein in his films and writings from the period 1923 to 1930.[4] Instead of maintaining narrative and spatial continuity between shots, as in the American style of editing, Eisenstein constructed his films (especially his earlier films) through a series of conflicting images. Editing, for Eisenstein, should not be fluid but shocking. He based his theory of editing on the same Hegelian dialectic that Marx used to formulate his theory of revolutionary change, and he believed that by combining two disparate shots (the first a thesis, the second its antithesis), a film could create a new concept (a synthesis) through the collision of images, a concept present in neither shot individually. To that end, he intersperses his earlier films with images that take spectators out of the immediately relevant narrative space to depict some other area or figure that offers a metaphorical accentuation or contrast to the narrative action. At other times, they show a character or an action from various discordant angles or drastically change the subject of the frame from one shot to the next. Eisenstein believed that incongruent combinations of shots would more effectively convey abstract ideas and create more passionate audience responses than the fluid "continuity editing" prominent in American cinema. He called his editing technique intellectual montage, and film scholars sometimes refer to it as "collision editing."

Raging Bull offers textbook illustrations of Eisenstein's editing method. Perhaps the most straightforward example of a single Eisensteinian edit is the cut from a scene between Jake and Vickie La Motta in their bedroom to a boxing scene between La Motta and Tony Janiro. In the bedroom scene, Jake questions a groggy Vickie about a comment she made about Janiro:

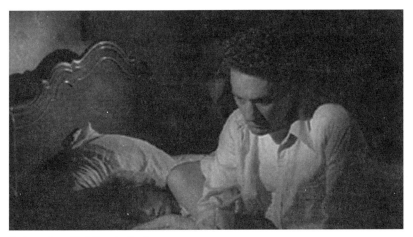

6. Low-key lighting in bedroom scene.

JAKE
Well, how come you said that thing about Janiro?

VICKIE
What'd I say?

JAKE
You said he had a pretty face.

VICKIE
I never noticed his face.

JAKE
Well, how come you said that then?

The scene is quiet (they speak softly, and we hear no ambient sounds or mood music) and the pace slow, but our knowledge of Jake's propensity for jealous violence makes the moment tense and pregnant with seething rage. The low-key lighting, which casts heavy shadows across their faces, makes the mood even more ominous (Figure 6). As the scene ends, we see Jake brooding on her comments.

Suddenly and shockingly, the film cuts to an extreme close-up of a boxer, presumably Janiro, getting punched twice in the face. The cut is precisely timed with the first punch, and we hear loud pummeling and a raucous crowd. The film makes no effort to smooth the harsh transition from the bedroom to the fighting ring: Instead, we move jarringly from a slow to a fast pace, from quiet to loudness, from

7a–d. Four consecutive shots from the eighth fight sequence, La Motta v. Robinson: **a)** Robinson's right jab; **b)** Reverse shot shows La Motta hit with a left hook; **c)** Robinson's right punch follows through; **d)** Jump-cut to low-angle shot of Robinson.

stillness to movement, and from contained violence to expressed violence. As Eisenstein would have predicted, the two shots, when combined, create a concept present in neither shot individually: La Motta uses boxing to express his anger and jealousy.

Scorsese peppers the fight sequences in *Raging Bull* with numerous visual collisions and cut-aways similar to the one that joins the bedroom scene to the Janiro fight. During the scene of La Motta's fight with Jimmy Reeves, for instance, the film cuts from the action

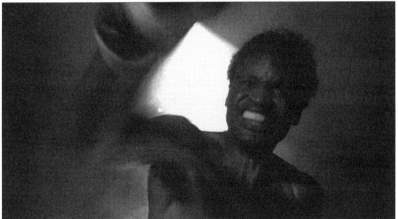

7a–d (*continued*).

in the ring to a shot of two men (one of them a soldier) fighting in
the stands. The juxtaposition of images suggests that the fighting in
the ring encourages and participates in a broader interest in violence
among boxing fans. The film extends that idea when it intersperses
shots of fans cheering the most brutal boxing activity, of photographers voyeuristically recording the bout, and of a riot among the fans
after the fight.

The most intensely Eisensteinian fight sequence is the title match
with Ray Robinson that results in La Motta's loss of the heavyweight
crown. During the final moments of the bout, Scorsese packs into

twenty-six seconds of screen time a sequence of thirty-five discordant shots that break fundamental rules of continuity editing to convey a subjective impression of La Motta's brutal experience in the ring.

As Robinson pummels La Motta, who is too tired even to defend himself, shots of the challenger's punches combine in a barrage of inconsistent images. For instance, Robinson's right jab in one shot (Figure 7a) illogically hits La Motta with a left hook in the subsequent shot (Figure 7b), and, when the film cuts back to Robinson, his right punch continues to follow through (Figure 7c). Violating the thirty-degree rule, the film then "jump-cuts" from the straight-on shot of Robinson (Figure 7c) to a low-angle shot of him (Figure 7d).[5] The sequence of thirty-five shots also contains nine violations of the 180-degree rule.[6]

As the sequence progresses from shot to shot, the camera angles and framing do not follow customary editing patterns. Indeed, the combination of shots seems almost random. Consider, for example, the violations of traditional continuity in the following seven shots. The angle on the action changes with each shot and – rather than only slightly shifting the frame's "center of interest," as is the custom in a conventionally edited sequence[7] – the film moves unpredictably from one close-up to another, drastically altering the subject of the frame with each cut.

Shot one: Low-angle extreme close-up of the front of Robinson's face.

Shot two: High-angle shot of La Motta's head and his left arm on the ropes.

Shot three: Close-up tracking down from La Motta's trunks to his bloody legs.

Shot four: Close-up of La Motta's face being punched.

Shot five: Extreme low-angle shot of Robinson's face.

Shot six: Extreme close-up of the left side of La Motta's face, slightly low-angle, as a glove hits his head.

Shot seven: Bird's-eye shot of Robinson's head and face.

Later, the sequence violates temporal and graphic continuity by portraying five successive shots of Robinson's gloves hitting La Motta's face, without any pause between punches, each shot from a different angle, two of them with the camera turned on its side at opposite ninety-degree angles (Figures 8a–b).

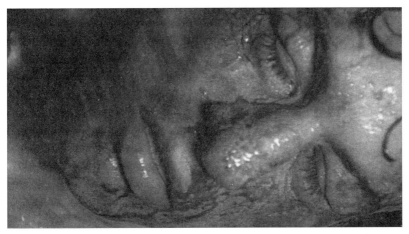

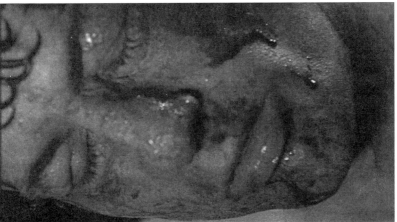

8. Two consecutive shots from the eighth fight sequence, La Motta v. Robinson.

Despite the continuity violations, the sequence does not feel as unconventional as comparable sequences from Eisenstein's films from the 1920s. Eisenstein often takes spectators out of the *diegesis* to create a symbolic association between juxtaposed images. In *October* (1927), for instance, he intercuts images of Kerensky with those of a mechanical peacock to suggest, through the visual metaphor, the Russian leader's pompousness and posturing.[8] The collision editing in *Raging Bull*, by contrast, is more consistent with continuity editing because it does not take the spectator out of the immediate space of the boxing ring. Moreover, as Hitchcock did in the shower sequence in *Psycho* (1960), Scorsese uses the jarring editing technique to convey the protagonist's subjective experience of the depicted violence: The rapid-fire and disorienting cuts convey the speed and impact of Robinson's blows. Scorsese said about this portion of the fight sequence, "It's not a matter of literally translating what Jake sees and hears, but to present what the match means for him, all the while respecting, as much as possible, historical truth" (*MSI*, 95). Eisenstein uses collision editing to convey all sorts of ideas, whereas here Scorsese, like Hitchcock, uses it to convey his protagonist's experience of violence.

VISUAL FLUIDITY AND *RAGING BULL*'S LONG STEADICAM SHOT

Scorsese relishes seamless visual transformations just as much as Eisensteinian collisions. Indeed, the director is known for his long, elegant tracking shots. *Goodfellas* (1990) uses three such shots: 1) Henry Hill's point-of-view shot as he enters a restaurant while characters introduce themselves directly to the camera; 2) the shot entering a refrigerated meat truck, which begins on a crane above the truck, slowly tracks through the truck's doors, weaves through hanging slabs of frozen meat, and finally stops tracking to film the frozen dead body of a mobster hanging on a meat hook; and 3) the shot of Henry and Karen entering the Copacabana night club, weaving their way through the back entrance, the hallways, the kitchen, and all the way to their seats, a shot in which the audience's aesthetic excitement mirrors Karen's excitement about her back-door entrance into the club and her date's astonishing privileges.

The long tracking shot of La Motta as he enters the ring before winning the middleweight crown from Marcel Cerdon rivals any of Scorsese's others in terms of its dramatic impact and dazzling display of virtuoso technique. For this extravagant shot, Scorsese and Chapman took advantage of the recently invented *Steadicam* camera-stabilizing system. First used commercially by Haskell Wexler in *Bound for Glory* (1976), the Steadicam enabled a camera operator to obtain smooth tracking shots using a handheld camera. It cut production costs by eliminating the need to lay tracks or use dollies or cranes and allowed operators to film more easily and smoothly in cars, on boats, moving up and down stairs, etc.[9] Scorsese and

Chapman also used the small, lightweight Arriflex 35 BL camera.[10] The Arriflex allowed them, without ballooning production costs, to create complex point-of-view shots and smooth tracking shots, to quickly reorient the camera in the middle of a shot, and to use makeshift rigs to, Scorsese has said, "get the cameras flying the way I wanted" (Kelly, 139).

The tracking shot of La Motta as he enters the ring takes full advantage of the beneficial features of the Steadicam and the lightweight Arriflex BL. I want to focus in particular on the ways in which the shot uses the rig's tractability and smoothness to cause the spectator to adopt the perspective of various "identities" that transform seamlessly as the camera progresses toward the fighting ring.

The shot begins in La Motta's dressing room where we see him warming up for the match (Figure 9a). The medium shot is confined by the dressing-room walls as well as by as the presence of Jake's brother Joey (Joe Pesci) and two trainers. The intimacy of the moment and the tightness of the shot align the spectator with La Motta's entourage, who watch him prepare for the most important fight of his career. As La Motta finishes donning his robe, the camera begins to track backward into the hallway outside the dressing room. During the backward tracking shot, we see Joey in the front of the frame, La Motta in the middle, and glimpses of the two trainers behind (Figure 9b). The shot of La Motta and his entourage, as the camera winds through the corridors, is familiar from numerous documentary films (such as *Don't Look Back* [1967] and *Richard Pryor: Live in Concert* [1979]) of singers and comedians as they enter an arena, and, at this point in the shot, the film adopts the look of a performance documentary. (*The Last Waltz*, Scorsese's 1978 documentary of the final concerts of The Band, contains a similar shot through the corridors of a recording studio.) The impression of a documentary film is strengthened when we start to see and hear fans cheering La Motta along, because in such films we generally feel we have privileged access to the performer, traveling with him as he moves through a crowd of fans (Figure 9c).

Soon, however, we seem to lose that sense of privilege and become one of those very fans. When the camera ducks into a corner and allows La Motta to pass, the backward tracking shot becomes, with hardly a pause, a forward tracking shot, and we now watch the back of the fighter while he enters the crowded arena, moving farther away

9a–e. Steadicam shots in *Raging Bull*: **a)** The green room; **b)** The corridor; **c)** Entering the arena; **d)** The man of the crowd; **e)** Within the ring.

9a–e (*continued*).

from us, as other fans increasingly block our view of him (Figure 9d).
As the shot tracks behind La Motta while he walks into the arena, we
see a huge, applauding crowd of spectators and an illuminated fight
ring in the distance. We can barely see La Motta as he jogs to the left
side of the ring and the camera moves to the right. Finally, the camera
sweeps into the air, filming the cheering crowd and the fighter as he
enters the ring (Figure 9e).[11] At this point, the camera is not limited
by the perspective of any individuals in the film, adopting instead the
perspective of an omniscient viewer, looking down on the dramatic
event. The moment is the visual antithesis of the confined frame

that began the shot, yet we have moved here without any abrupt transitions. As the camera takes on its various identities – La Motta's entourage, performance-documentary filmmaker, boxing fan, omniscient viewer – the transformations are always fluid, and one could not demarcate the frames in which each change occurred.

The fluid style of the tracking shot that joins Jake's dressing room to the fight ring precisely opposes that of the jarring Eisensteinian cuts used to construct the pummeling sequence of the final La Motta/Robinson match. Scorsese's film combines these antithetical styles (along with several other styles), sometimes within individual scenes. To understand the ways in which *Raging Bull* harmonizes its disparate imagery, we should turn to the film's opening moments, whose visual style is an emblem for that of the entire film. From its very first shots, *Raging Bull* seems to be falling apart stylistically, whereas a range of visual unifiers hold together the film's disintegrating pieces.

FALLING APART LIKE JAKE?

THE FIRST SEVEN SHOTS OF *RAGING BULL*

The first seven shots of *Raging Bull* present three stylistically discordant moments: a dream-like sequence of La Motta shadowboxing, a more documentary-like scene of the aging boxer in a nightclub dressing room, and the intense first fight sequence between La Motta and Jimmy Reeves. Scorsese structures the movements from shot to shot around a series of sharp contrasts (contrasting imagery, tones, and ideas) that create an Eisensteinian sense of graphic contradiction and collision, meanwhile smoothing over the contrasts with narratively incidental elements that help to harmonize the visual conflicts and link the incongruously presented spaces.

In the film's first shot (after three title cards), we see a fighter shadowboxing in a ring, the opening credits laid on top of the frame. The black-and-white, slow-motion shot romanticizes the boxer. He moves with dance-like grace as his leopard-patterned robe gently billows around him, flashbulbs lighting in an airy mist surrounding the boxing ring. The intermezzo from Mascagni's romantic *Cavalleria Rusticana* plays in the soundtrack. The sequence instills boxing with a sense of lonely grandeur, as the solitary fighter dances around the ring in what metaphorically suggests a warm-up before a bout.[12]

Nine seconds after the end of the credit sequence, the film makes a striking transition to a shot of Robert De Niro as the aging former middleweight champion rehearsing a poem in his dressing room for a nightclub performance. In this fifth shot of the movie, an older-looking, grotesquely overweight De Niro appears in stark contrast to the graceful, svelte, and youthful actor of the credits. (The image of De Niro in this shot is made more jarring – and becomes, in 1980, immediately famous – because the actor himself has clearly gained so much weight for the role, pushing method acting to extraordinary lengths.) The lighting in the dressing room, moreover, looks hard and realistic, compared with the soft, misty lighting during the credit sequence. Whereas the first shot was romantic and ethereal, shot five appears drab and documentary-like.

The film smoothes the progression from shot one to shot five with several unifying elements. For one thing, the movement from the credits to narrative action has occurred gradually: Shot one depicts title credits that display writing outside of the story's *diegesis;* shot two is an intertitle that also displays non-*diegetic* writing ("New York City, 1964"), but that refers to story information; and shots three and four depict a street signboard that displays text that appears within the diegetic space of the movie:

An Evening with Jake La Motta
    Tonight 8:30

Hence, the film takes spectators from outside the story to the story's interior through four successive shots of written text, and it feels like a natural progression when the fifth shot begins depicting narrative action. Other elements unify the first five shots of the movie. The idea of *preparation for a public performance* joins the shot of La Motta warming up in the ring to the shot of him rehearsing in his dressing room, and both shots reveal La Motta as a solitary, even lonely, figure. Moreover, the image of the younger La Motta shadowboxing reverberates with the poem the older La Motta recites that recalls his previous boxing career, "I remember those cheers, they still ring in my ears." Finally, La Motta's spoken lines extend over the cut from the shots of the signboard to that of the dressing room, providing a sound bridge from shot three to shot five.

The dressing-room scene, which lasts about one minute, cuts abruptly to a boxing scene that takes place twenty-three years earlier and that could hardly be more disparate in style and tone. Scorsese, however, maintains several graphic consistencies across the cut from

the sixth shot of the film (the final shot of the dressing room sequence) to the seventh (the opening shot of the film's first boxing
sequence). A medium close-up of the older La Motta in his dressing
room (Figure 10) cuts to an almost identically framed medium close-
up of a younger La Motta fighting in the ring (Figure 11), and the
words "Jake La Motta 1941" in shot seven replace "Jake La Motta,
1964" in shot six. Several other consistencies join the two shots. A
metal bar behind La Motta in the dressing room graphically matches
the ropes behind him in the fighting ring. La Motta, moreover, still
appears alone in the frame, and his spoken line, "That's entertainment," extends over the cut, providing another sound bridge. Scorsese said that he discovered the cut from the dressing room scene to
the first fight sequence "by accident one night at the editing table,
when I was in despair about being able to connect Jake's bloated face
of the 60s with his young face of the 1940s. Two tracks accidentally
overlapped and bang!" (*MSI*, 93). Shot seven also recalls prior shots
in the film: The appearance of written text, "Jake La Motta 1941"
(which uses the same non-serif, shadowed, all-capital-letter font of
the credits), echoes the appearance of text in five earlier shots, and
the shot of La Motta in the ring connects it to the shot of the same
lean, young boxer of the credit sequence.

Nonetheless, the cut to shot seven is extremely jarring. The young
La Motta looks trim and focused (Figure 11), as opposed to the portly,
slightly stuttering La Motta of the dressing-room scene (Figure 10).
The tone of the film has moved from quiet to loud, from dispassion-
ate to intense, and from placid to brutal. Indeed, as soon as the older
La Motta completes his line, "That's entertainment," the young La
Motta twice gets punched in the face. Shot seven, moreover, has none
of the ethereal beauty of the credit sequence that it recalls, depicting
boxing not with romance and grandeur but with brutality. Indeed,
the credit sequence contains the only images in the movie in which
La Motta's boxing talents appear graceful.

The entirety of *Raging Bull* works similarly to its first seven shots.
On the one hand, *Raging Bull*'s disparate styles and colliding images threaten the film with visual incoherence. The film, for instance, mixes home-movie-style color footage (spliced into each exhibition print *by hand* because the footage used different print stock),
still photography, intertitles, and television footage. Moreover, the

10. Shot six of *Raging Bull*.

stylization and visual complexity of the fight sequences contrast with the documentary-like realism of the sequences outside the ring, which, aside from occasional slow-motion effects and heavily low-key lighting, mostly employ straightforward conventions of lighting, editing, and cinematography.

On the other hand, the film's various harmonizing elements provide continuities from shot to shot and throughout the film. For example, the black-and-white cinematography creates high-contrast images and dramatic shadows in sequences both inside and outside

11. Shot seven of *Raging Bull*.

the ring and gives much of *Raging Bull* the look of film noir as well as 1940s press photography, both of which, according to Chapman, influenced the film's visual style.[13] Moreover, although each fight sequence is shot in a distinct style, all of them keep the camera mostly inside the ring, and most make use of slow-motion cinematography, extreme high- and low-angle shots, and zooms or moving cameras. Furthermore, most of the fight sequences include shots of smoke-filled arenas, heated discussions between La Motta and his crew in his corner, and photojournalists incessantly snapping photographs.[14] The film also feels stabilized by a narrative purpose that generally conforms to principles of classical Hollywood narration, at least in the first hour and twenty minutes: Our protagonist has a clearly defined goal (to win the middleweight championship) and must overcome obstacles (mobsters, a boxing scandal, weight problems, and arguments with his brother and wives) to achieve it in a definitive climax (the 1949 Cerdon fight).[15] Consequently, although *Raging Bull* often risks stylistic disharmony in precarious ways, one generally experiences the film not as avant-garde experiment or salmagundi but as unified.

In the next, final section of this essay, I want to show that *Raging Bull* takes its visual disharmony even to the point of absurdity. I want also to show, however, that the film prevents spectators from recognizing the disharmony and absurdity *as* disharmony and absurdity and enables them to make sense out of visually nonsensical information.

ON THE BRINK OF ABSURDITY: "LA MOTTA VS. SUGAR RAY ROBINSON, DETROIT 1943"

The film's depiction of the first 1943 bout between La Motta and Robinson best illustrates the extent to which *Raging Bull* courts visual and logical incoherence. I propose to study that incoherence without, as other scholars attempt to do, making it seem more coherent. Robin Wood, for instance, wants to "make sense" of the film's incoherent structure to "explain the fascination that La Motta and the film hold for our culture."[16] Instead, I want to show that our culture's fascination with *Raging Bull* results at least partly from the impossibility of making the film make sense.[17]

The entire bout takes 75 seconds of screen time, but three shots that depict La Motta punching Robinson out of the boxing ring are particularly dense with illogic; they last five seconds. After describing the sequence of shots, I shall attempt to demonstrate that spectators understand the sequence despite that much of what they understand is plainly absurd.

Shot one (Figure 12a). Low-angle long shot of La Motta driving Robinson from the right side of the ring to the left as the camera tracks left with them.

Shot two (Figures 12b–d). High-angle, over-the-shoulder shot as La Motta punches Robinson out of the ring (Figure 12b). The shot is in fast motion, and the camera quickly zooms in from a long shot of Robinson to a medium close-up, as the boxer falls to the floor beyond the ring (Figure 12c). The camera then tilts up to film a photojournalist taking a flash photograph from ringside. The frame then turns almost completely white, and, as the whiteness fades, we see the decaying flash of the photographer's camera (Figure 12d).

Shot three (Figure 12e). A freeze-frame representing a still photograph, brightly lit, taken from ringside, presumably the photograph taken by the photographer in shot two. La Motta has just punched Robinson, who is in the midst of falling out of the ring.

This dense and rapid series of shots asks an audience to understand a lot that does not make sense. Let's begin with the most illogical shot in the sequence – shot three (Figure 12e), the brightly lit still frame of La Motta punching Robinson out of the ring. The shot invites spectators to understand that the photograph taken by the photojournalist in shot two has been developed and is presumably printed in a newspaper the following day. Compounding the temporal displacement, the picture depicts Robinson in mid-air, even though shot two showed the boxer already on the ground (Figure 12c). Hence, the one-second still shot moves our minds both forward in time (to the next-day's newspaper) and backward (to before Robinson hit the ground) at the same instant.

The sequence's most unfeasible ideas, however, result from our likely impression that the photographer represented in the left side of shot three (Figure 12c) is the same photographer depicted in shot two (Figure 12d), in other words the same photographer who presumably *took* shot three, the very shot in which he appears.

12a–e. The consecutive shots from the first 1943 bout between La Motta and Robinson.

12a–e (*continued*).

It would be perfectly logical to assume that we are looking at a photograph taken by a photographer we have not seen. However, I doubt audiences *do* assume so, because the conventions of continuity editing – which help orient us during the rapid cuts – tell us that the same photographer who is in the picture also took it. On the one hand, the convention of the eyeline match (when one shot depicts someone looking at something and the subsequent shot shows what the person sees) suggests that, when a shot of a photojournalist taking a photograph (shot two) is followed by the shot of a photograph (shot three), the photojournalist (in shot two) must have taken the photograph (shot three). On the other hand, the convention of the graphic match (when two consecutive shots contain similar graphic elements) tells us that the photographers depicted in the two shots (who look the same and are performing the very same action in what looks like the very same location) are the same. Although, in this instance, the different editing conventions result in an illogical idea, I suspect one would find it more difficult to mentally insert a new photographer into the sequence than to allow the matches to orient us from shot to shot. In other words, spectators probably prefer nonsense to disorientation, as long as they don't recognize the nonsense *as* nonsense.

Several explanations might account for the feeling of coherence that a close analysis of the series of frames belies. For one thing, the brevity of the sequence invites spectators to make whatever sense they can out of the barrage of images, and, as the narrative moves quickly forward, one need not bother figuring out the details of the various temporal and spatial impossibilities. The sequence, moreover, does not *evidently* fail to make sense unless one thinks about it, because spectators would only find themselves presented with the inconceivable notion that the photographer has taken his own picture if they connected two separate assumptions: 1) that the photographer in shot two took the picture in shot three, and 2) that the figure of the photographer and his camera in shot three coincides with similar figures in shot two. The incompatibility of the two assumptions does not prevent them from seeming independently correct. Moreover, the narrative (the film's most forceful unifier), and our investment in our protagonist's efforts to win the bout, provide a stable context capable of distracting us from the film's lapses in visual coherence.

The depiction of the 1943 bout contains several other elements that flirt almost as boldly with visual absurdity. For instance, although filmmakers generally reserve fast motion for comic sequences in movies (such as Keystone Cops chase sequences) and transitions (such as in *Zazie dans le Métro* [1960]), shot two (Figures 12b–d) uses the technique during a moment of serious dramatic action. Later, after Robinson gets up from the floor, we see La Motta walking back to his corner of the ring. The shot of La Motta begins in real time, moves into slow motion, and then returns to real time again, a stylistic strangeness that is only partly excused by the impression that the film has adopted the subjectivity of La Motta, impatiently waiting for Robinson to stand up and return to the fight.[18]

Some of the most absurd moments in the scene combine images and sounds in a bizarre way. Whereas the sounds of punches and cheering fans provide a degree of realism – as does the radio announcer's commentary, which also supplies pertinent story information ("The undefeated Sugar Ray and the defeated Jake at Madison Square Garden," "in the first knock-down of his career," etc.) – nonetheless, we also hear narratively incongruous sounds that come across almost comically in the context of a boxing match: booming sounds (like a large animal thumping in the forest), something that sounds to me like an elephant screaming, and a high-pitched screech that fades into the sounds of cheering fans.[19]

One six-second shot contains some of the scene's strangest imagery and sounds. At first tracking La Motta as he punches Robinson from the left side of the ring to the right (Figure 13a), the camera then tilts up disorientingly and whip pans across the lights of the arena (Figure 13b). Nothing within the narrative motivates the camera's tilt upward (none of the characters, for instance, looks up into the arena's rafters to provide a narrative "excuse" for filming there), and it feels momentarily reassuring when it tilts back down to the ring, where one expects it to land on Robinson. Instead, it lands on La Motta (Figure 13c), who now faces the opposite direction and drives Robinson to the *left* side of the ring. The boxers apparently changed places when the camera filmed the lights, and it takes a moment for us to reorient to their new locations. Even more bizarre, as the camera tilts up to the lights and then back down, we hear something that resembles the revving sound of a cartoon character winding up for a punch.

Scenes such as the one depicting the 1943 bout between La Motta and Robinson seem intent upon including elements that threaten to make the film absurd and that complicate what would otherwise be a straightforward exposition of the story. The film invites spectators to integrate into their general experience of the scene effects impertinent to the scene's narrative purpose.

13a–c. A single, six-second shot from the first 1943 bout between La Motta and Robinson: **a)** La Motta lands a right; **b)** Disorientation; **c)** La Motta and Robinson have now changed places.

The unobtrusive nonsense of *Raging Bull* differs from conspicuously anti-verisimilar aspects in some art films, such as visual distortions in *The Cabinet of Dr. Caligari* (1919), temporal and spatial illogic in *October*, narrative nonsense in *Last Year at Marienbad* (1961), or the various absurdities of style and character behavior in *Pierrot le Fou* (1965). Such films advertise their violations of logic and conventional realism and are therefore confined by the limitations imposed on anything (even distortions and paradoxes) that can be fixed and categorized. Watching *Raging Bull*, we understand what we see without noticing that logic would prevent us from understanding it. Because the film seems coherent but is not, it remains a step removed from perfect intelligibility, and one's efforts to understand it only make the film feel more elusive. Critics often call *Raging Bull* complex, but its complexity is partly an effect of contradiction and absurdity masquerading as coherence. The film seems to have more going on than it really has.

Sequences like the 1943 match between La Motta and Robinson make sense only because we *want* them to make sense and because incidental harmonies encourage us to temper, disregard, or make do with the film's various absurdities. It takes a confident filmmaker – confident in his talents as well as in the audience's ability to process complex visual information – to flirt so boldly with incoherence. However, although at times *Raging Bull* seems held together only by weak stitching, the stability offered by its various visual and narrative unities prevents it from separating into incoherent pieces.[20] The film invites audiences to conform it to the logic of its more conventional and harmonious features – classical narration, continuity editing, graphic unities – which provide a solid backdrop against which Scorsese can lay his visual anarchy. Hence, *Raging Bull* asks spectators to perform mental activities more athletic than those performed when watching more coherent works of art: It asks them to make order out of the barrage of chaos the film insists on hitting them with. Spectators do not simply fill in gaps the movie leaves open. To understand what they are watching, they must mentally correct the movie so that it depicts not what reason says it is depicting but rather what narrative context says it *must* be depicting. Hence, they make *Raging Bull* into something logic insists it is not: coherent and comprehensible.

NOTES

1. Qtd. in James Naremore, ed. *North by Northwest* (New Brunswick: Rutgers University Press, 1993), 181.
2. Several scholars have discussed the film's lack of narrative coherence. For example, Robin Wood, *Hollywood from Vietnam to Reagan* (New York: Columbia University Press, 1986), 251, writes, "The film's fragmented structure can be read as determined by La Motta's own incoherence, by Scorsese's fascination with that incoherence and with the violence that is its product." Marie Katheryn Connelly, *Martin Scorsese: An Analysis of His Feature Films, with a Filmography of His Entire Directorial Career* (Jefferson, NC: McFarland, 1991), 73, calls the film's structure fragmentary: "Conventional transitions are not provided, and viewers must actively participate in pulling together the materials for themselves and coming to an understanding of the meaning of what has been presented."
3. Andy Dougan, *Martin Scorsese* (New York: Thunder's Mouth Press, 1998), 93–94.
4. David Bordwell, "Eisenstein's Epistemological Shift," *Screen* 15, no. 4 (1974–1975): 34–41, draws a distinction between the early theoretical writings of Eisenstein during the 1923–1930 period, which emphasized a montage of contradiction and collision, and those of the 1930–1948 period, which more greatly emphasized synthesis. Bordwell sees a "Romantic aesthetic" in the later writings and films, when Eisenstein embraces "synethesia or 'syncronisation of senses' in accordance with a new theory of the art work: the work as a polyphonic tissue of interwoven 'lines.'"
5. The thirty-degree rule instructs filmmakers to vary the camera position from shot to shot by at least thirty degrees. Violating the rule results in a jump-cut.
6. The 180-degree rule helps to maintain clear and consistent screen space. See David Bordwell and Kristin Thompson, *Film Art: An Introduction*, 6th ed. (New York: McGraw-Hill, 2001), 263.
7. Moving from one shot to the next in a classical Hollywood movie, according to David Bordwell, "tonality, movement, and the center of compositional interest shift enough to be distinguishable but not enough to be disturbing." See David Bordwell, Janet Staiger, and Kristin Thompson, *The Classical Hollywood Cinema: Film Style and Mode of Production to 1960* (London: Routledge, 1988), 55.
8. Bordwell, "Eisenstein's Epistemological Shift," 36, writes that "the bird's stiff movements (it is a *clockwork* peacock) announce the link between Kerensky and those mechanical artifacts that inhabit the Winter Palace."
9. For general information on the development of the Steadicam and the Arriflex, see David Cook, *Lost Illusions: American Cinema in the Shadow of Watergate and Vietnam, 1970–1979* (New York: Charles Scribner's Sons, 2000), 371–376.
10. Michael Chapman was particularly pleased to be able to use new Zeiss lenses: "The thing, more or less new I guess, for which I was most grateful on the technological front, was the wonderful set of Zeiss Super Speeds with which

we shot [*Taxi Driver* and *Raging Bull*]. They were amazingly accurately cali-
brated so that 2.8 was really 2.8 and 1.9 really 1.9. Most lenses are nowhere
near so true." Michael Chapman, e-mail to author, 6 November 2001.

11.   Chapman described how he got the camera into the air in the last moments
      of the Steadicam shot as follows: "The Steadicam operator stepped onto a
      platform rigged on a stage crane which was wheeled into position when the
      lens had passed it and it thus wouldn't be seen. Then as Bobby [De Niro]
      walked away and climbed into the ring the grips simply raised the crane
      and, as I remember, swung it to the right." Michael Chapman, e-mail to the
      author, 7 July 2003.

12.   Connelly, *Martin Scorsese*, 74, says about this shot, "The slow motion softens
      his punches, effecting a grace and lyricism."

13.   To prepare for black-and-white shooting, Chapman and Scorsese screened
      Double Indemnity (1944) and *The Sweet Smell of Success* (1957), as well as Buster
      Keaton shorts. Chapman says that he also studied tabloid photography from
      the 1940s to determine the look of *Raging Bull*: "The '40s were the great days
      of press photography, like the *New York Daily News* and *Life* magazine and
      photojournalism in the grand manner that we no longer have. And many
      of the great subjects of that time were prizefighters. There were many, many
      photographs of Jake La Motta, for example. He was a very popular subject
      in his day. So it appeared to Marty and me that this kind of look embodied
      a certain kind of spirit, of the way those people looked at the world." Qtd.
      in Ric Gentry, "Michael Chapman Captures *Raging Bull* in Black and White,"
      Millimeter 9 (February 1981): 112.

      Scorsese has indicated several reasons for shooting *Raging Bull* in black and
      white: He was concerned about the tendency of color-film stock to fade; he
      wanted to give the movie the feeling of a documentary and to differentiate
      his film from several other boxing pictures coming out at the same time in
      the wake of *Rocky* (1976), including *Rocky II, The Champ, The Main Event*,
      and *Matilda*; and black and white recalls boxing pictures from the era in
      which in film primarily takes place, such as *Body and Soul* (1947) and *The Set-
      Up* (1949). Chapman offers a somewhat different account: "I wanted to [film
      black and white] out of craftsmanship, for professional reasons. And [Scorsese
      is] an old film scholar and film obsessive; many of the films he grew up on
      were in black and white. So when he called me about *Raging Bull*, we agreed
      that this was our chance." Qtd. in Gentry, "Michael Chapman Captures,"
      108–109.

14.   Chapman says, "There were enormous and elaborately choreographed flash-
      bulb sequences, where the flashes go off all around the boxers in spirals, or
      shot at 120 frames with just the flashes so it would be like strobe lighting, an
      incessant beat that became very abstract, as it did in the last fight with Sugar
      Ray Robinson." Qtd. in Gentry, "Michael Chapman Captures," 114. Gentry,
      115, adds that the flashes are "extremely effective at punctuating the drama
      of the fight, and likewise casting behind and around the fighters an aura of
      light that is simultaneously reminiscent of released kinetic energy through
      their violent interaction, as well as a wavering spiritual pulse."

15. David Bordwell, "Classical Hollywood Cinema: Narrational Principles and Procedures," *Narrative, Apparatus, Ideology*, ed. Philip Rosen (New York: Columbia University Press, 1986), 18, writes, "The classical Hollywood film presents psychologically defined individuals who struggle to solve a clear-cut problem or to attain specific goals. In the course of this struggle, the characters enter into conflict with others or with external circumstances. The story ends with a decisive victory or defeat, a resolution of the problem and a clear achievement or nonachievement of the goals."

16. Wood, *Hollywood from Vietnam to Reagan*, 251.

17. My discussion of the aesthetic value of nonsense is indebted to Stephen Booth's *Precious Nonsense: The Gettysburg Address, Ben Jonson's Epitaphs on His Children, and Twelfth Night* (Berkeley: University of California Press, 1998). Booth, 35–36, writes that great works of art "are, and seem often to work hard at being, always on the point of one or another kind of incoherence – always on the point of disintegrating and/or integrating the very particulars they exclude."

18. Scorsese said that he came up with the idea of sliding into slow motion on the set: "At that point, we overcranked, so that it was normal, twenty-four frames; and then we went to forty-eight within the shot so it became slow motion; then back to twenty-four as he came around to his corner, the neutral corner, to wait. Then bang, cut, and he came back in fighting. That we did on the set" (Kelly, 136).

19. Donald O. Mitchell, a sound re-recording engineer for *Raging Bull*, said that sound-effects editor Frank Warner used "animal sounds such as a lion roar mixed over a man's scream." David Weishaar, "Interview with Donald O. Mitchell (Part 1)," 9 September 2003, *FilmSound.org*, <www.filmsound.org/cas/mitchell1.htm>. Scorsese said about Warner, "He used rifle shots and melons breaking, but he wouldn't tell us what many of the effects were; he became very possessive and even burnt them afterwards so nobody else could use them" (*SS*, 83).

20. Booth, *Precious Nonsense*, 35, writes, "Great works of art are daredevils. They flirt with disasters and, at the same time, they let you know they are married forever to particular, reliable order and purpose."

3 *Raging Bull* and the Idea of Performance

Performance studies can offer film studies much. Seen from the perspective of this emerging field of studies, *Raging Bull* becomes an even more complex work. Answers to such questions as who is performing and what is being performed are far from simple. As the opening sequence suggests, *Raging Bull* makes the idea of performance a predominant theme. The film examines how masculinity is performed within the boxing arena and without. In so doing, it begs comparison with the great stage plays of the mid-twentieth century that also interrogate the performance of masculinity. As a biographical film of a performer, *Raging Bull* shows Robert De Niro performing as Jake La Motta performing as both a boxer and as a stand-up comedian. Incorporating Brando's famous speech from *On the Waterfront* (1954) near its end, *Raging Bull* adds further layers of performance: De Niro as Jake as Brando as Terry Malloy. Through allusion and homage, this closing scene has been re-performed numerous times since the film's release, and additional layers of complexity accumulate as *Raging Bull* gathers history.

BEGINNING BETWEEN DOING AND SEEMING

Raging Bull begins with a very specific circumstance of performance. In the opening title sequence, a boxer spars with the smokey air in an empty ring. Only vague movements are visible from those just outside the ropes; flashbulbs occasionally burst through the gloom. The three ropes on the camera's side of the ring divide the frame into four horizontal strips, so that the screen looks almost like a musical staff across which the boxer moves (Figure 14). In crafting the opening as a slow-motion dance-like solo sequence, not at first clearly integrated to the narrative, Martin Scorsese positions his protagonist between the two extremes of performance towards which character, actor and director are so violently drawn throughout the film. On the one hand, the boxer is pretending to box (perhaps he is even "showing off" for his fans or attempting to intimidate his opponent, but the shot certainly does not emphasize this). He mimes fighting, he *rehearses*. On the other hand, the boxer simply does what boxers do before a fight. Not "rehearsal" but *practice*. The film begins poised between seeming and doing.

The sequence also establishes a dramatic situation that is not yet a drama – a boxing ring floating in space (it soon will be fixed in the narrative as the site of La Motta's first loss – on points – to Jimmy Reeves, but not before the film flashes *forward* to its ending). The beginning passage functions as a tableau, an abstracted image, even if in retrospect we know that the film is actually starting *in media res*. The scene also cues the viewer to expect seriousness. It is the first of innumerable instances of beautiful black and white cinematography, and the score – the intermezzo of the short opera *Cavalleria Rusticana* – lends the opening an elegiac tone. The title sequence offers an interpretive hint, in positioning the boxer not in an expository, explanatory frame, but as a lonely and unknowable hooded figure. It also exemplifies the most tenable position from which to observe the hero: at a healthy aestheticizing distance. The pleasures of contemplating the unnamed, ahistorical boxer from this remove are soon and repeatedly established through contrast with bloody close-ups, which dominate the actual fight sequences.

It is not even the character, the protagonist Jake La Motta, who is so poised on the cusp of fictional and efficacious performance – not yet. To be sure, the actor De Niro is, in this sequence, already transformed. His slow dance for the camera, especially when viewed with two decades of hindsight, illustrates the actor's accomplishment, his almost sacrificial becoming-boxer that is so much a part of the mythology of the film. But the choreography communicates more about boxing – and about acting – than about character at this point. De Niro's face is hooded by the leopard-print robe that will

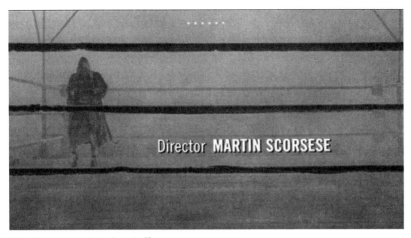

14. Shot one of *Raging Bull.*

(only later) help to delineate the somewhat ridiculous theatricality surrounding La Motta. His face recedes, his feet and his hands holding the eye instead. We see a boxer, but not yet the Bronx Bull. It is not that the moment is somehow prior to acting, but that *in it the action of the boxer and that of the actor are identical.* In the build-up to the film's release, La Motta suggested that De Niro, having trained with him, could be a ranking middleweight. Perhaps inadvertently, Scorsese's opening abets the lionizing of the star of a film that in its later sequences both humanizes and animalizes the character he plays.

Although this most beautiful passage of the film has it both ways in celebrating seemingly opposed vectors of performance, *Raging Bull* as a whole is uncertain about the merits of cultural versus forceful performance. The film's work engages its ambivalence to violence, masculinity, and society *through* performance. The opening scene does not resolve these tensions, and if it seems like a paradise from which the film falls, this is a function of its naivete rather than its innocence. The opening looks at performance from a formal, ahistorical perspective, before the film has broached the contradictions within society and character. It finds a beautiful and oddly peaceful accommodation of multiple performance imperatives.

My reading lingers over this scene, as *Raging Bull* does. The next two scenes are crucially and excruciatingly joined by an overlap of sound and image. In the following scene, we see the aging, over-weight La Motta rehearsing the lines of his nightclub act backstage (Figure 15). His rote memorization is not compelling, though it bears some resemblance to a boxer's sparring by himself. La Motta's recitation ends with the line "That's entertainment" – a showbiz bit, the most workaday kind of reflexivity. The view then cuts to a closeup of Jake's face in the ring. Just as he repeats, "That's entertainment," the first punch hits him, launching the initial frenetic fight scene.

In moments like this, *Raging Bull* constructs a dramatic irony central to its meaning. The film shares with its audience an insight La Motta cannot (at least at first) admit: that real combat and the seeming falsity of entertainment are as much alike as different. *Raging Bull* juxtaposes La Motta's *athletic* performance as a fighter with his later *cultural* performances as a celebrity attraction. His athletic performance is driven by the masculine animal power suggested by the title, whereas his stand-up appearances imply a pitiable reduction and confinement of his beastly side. His movement from *doer* to *actor* is a shift from one sense of performance to another. The film sympathizes with Jake's initial insistence on the purity of his effort, endurance, and competition, but *Raging Bull* also sees "realistically" the unavoidable proximity of the two modes.

It may be that *Raging Bull*, like so many investigations of masculinity, ultimately functioned regressively. One straightforward critique is that the film celebrates the exploits of an admitted fight-fixer, batterer, and rapist. Whether the portrait of the boxer is seen as celebratory or cautionary, the film can be read conveniently and coherently as a tragedy of macho purity dragged down by the falsity of the modern world. As such, it is clearly recuperable to a sexist historical narrative that pities men as heroic victims of shifts in economic and cultural production. In Pam Cook's terms, "masculinity is put into crisis so that we can mourn its loss."[1] This seems to me a strong, but flexible summary of the film's emotional force, though Judith Halberstam's observation that it is "hard to be very concerned about the burden of masculinity on males, however, if only because it so often expresses itself through the desire to destroy others, often women" is apt here and goes to the heart of the matter.[2] The film by no means ignores the pain inflicted on others by Jake's masculinity crisis, but this is "collateral damage" rendered to intensify the

15. Too much linguine.

tragedy of the central character. Still, to flesh out the analysis of its depictions of masculinity, bloodsport, and modernity necessitates asking more than whether the film "glorifies" a violent and at times corrupt fighter, and whether La Motta is depicted as an "uncompromising" exemplar of natural masculinity; we need to parse the film's own theorizing of athletic and artistic performance.

THE KING OF TRAGEDY

The construction of most serious movies of this period is far different from the shape of acclaimed semi-realistic American stage drama of the mid-century, such as *A View From the Bridge* (1955) or *Death of A Salesman* (1949). Most obviously, *Raging Bull* favors an episodic structure in which the protagonist's falling to pieces happens *in* pieces rather than with the typical satisfactions of a clear dramatic climax. When used in the context of drama criticism, "cinematic" usually means just such an aesthetic of spatial and temporal flow as that which marks this film.

Given their differing structures, then, the simple reason that so many would identify both these acclaimed stage plays and Scorsese's film as "tragedies" lies in a commonsense understanding of tragedy as having an unhappy ending in which the mighty are brought low. Beyond this, however, *Raging Bull* also offers a sense of social drama similar to that Arthur Miller described in his attempt to revise tragic theory in his essay "Tragedy and the Common Man." Jake, like Miller's patriarchs, could be seen as a protagonist who struggles to maintain a traditional understanding of his identity in the face of modernity, who tries to "evaluate himself justly" even though he does not see clearly the rules under which he plays.[3] In Scorsese's words, "I understand that several sportswriters have said we've glorified a fight fixer. There is no glorification, and whether he fixed a fight or not doesn't matter. What we had is a picture of a man who didn't compromise."[4]

Like Miller's salesman Willy Loman, Jake both fails to live up to his own sense of rightness and fails to fully understand the system against which he attempts to rebel. This comparison holds to varying degrees across all of Scorsese and De Niro's early works exploring performance. *The King of Comedy* (1982), for example, makes clear their interest in transgressive bad performers who don't know they are bad, but even aspects of De Niro's other characters, as in *Taxi Driver*, display incompetent social performance.

In both *Death of a Salesman* and *All My Sons* (1947), the protagonist confronts both his own failed rightness and his previous misunderstanding of his social system – precipitating his suicide. In *Raging Bull*, Jake's similar realization appears to come in the very late scene of his solitary confinement in a Florida jail; however, it leads not to death, but to show business. La Motta is in jail after he fails to raise the bribe money he believes will "fix" his morals charge, but the deputies' comments suggest that he is being put in solitary for "shirking" on his work detail – yet another scene of punishment for refusal to perform. When the deputies force him into the cell, La Motta calls himself "dummy, dummy" and head butts and punches the wall repeatedly. He cries "they called me an animal. I'm not an animal... I'm not that guy." In struggling subsequently to build a second career as an entertainer, is Jake defying, or capitulating to, the society that brought him to this nadir?

Although Jake never moves into the role of father so central to Miller's drama, he shares other affinities with the dramatist's heroes, especially with the Italian immigrant dockworker of Brooklyn's Red Hook depicted in *A View from the Bridge*. Notable in both works is a connection between irrational sexual jealousy and homosexual desire, made explicit in Miller's play but visible in *Raging Bull* primarily in the frequent homophobic remarks, including Jake's striking put-down of Janiro, "I got a problem whether I should fuck him or fight him."

What this comparison clarifies is the degree to which the film's meaning is dependent on its protagonist's ignorance or naivete. La Motta's desire for a clearly defined and potent masculinity are incommensurable, not just with the corruption of the modern world, but with the laws of physics and his own contradictory feelings. He doesn't understand why he should be physically fated never to fight the heavyweight champion Joe Louis, which he recognizes in studying his own "little girl's hands." When he asks Joey to hit him in the head, he apparently doesn't know the answer to his brother's question, "What're you trying to prove?" and can only answer by provoking through an attack on his hetero-masculinity: "You throw a punch like you take it up the ass."

(The pervasive homophobic dialogue in *Raging Bull* marks an important difference from Miller's view of tragic American masculinity. The protagonist of *A View from the Bridge* struggles simply, and alone, against his attraction to another man – it is, in a perhaps unintentionally homophobic dramaturgy, his tragic flaw. In contrast, Scorsese focuses on a milieu defined by a generalized [articulated through explicit homophobia] *positive* construction of masculinity. Positive, that is, in that homosocial but heterosexist masculine culture is collaboratively built, in this world, through casual homophobic behavior. In Miller's Italian-American tragedy, homosexuality is the problem, whereas in Scorsese's, homophobia is one kind of solution. This aspect, however, is complicated by the thoroughly erotic visuality of the film, such that La Motta's disavowal [through homophobia] becomes the film's invitation to diverse sexualized ways of looking.)

Most importantly for the "tragic" structure of the film, Jake senses that boxing and show business are related, but he can't manage that relationship. He alternately denies it and embraces it. Jake is churlish toward journalists early in the film, yet near the end the retired boxer uses a press photographer to record family scenes of his wife and children by his swimming pool. In the ring, he stubbornly resists playing the game that fight-fixers expect as part of progress toward a championship match, yet in the very first fight scene he betrays a concern with appearances as he snaps at his corner-men to "put my robe on right. Put it on right!" (In the previous scene, the flash-forward to his rehearsal in the dressing room, Jake recites a poem that begins with the memory of cheers from the crowd, followed by the statement that one night he entered the ring and removed his robe to discover he'd forgotten to wear shorts.)

Jake's confusion and ambivalence about the relationship of sport and mimesis crystalizes around the question of the authenticity of violence. From an athletic viewpoint, La Motta's career, as depicted in the film, is in fact characterized by his *refusal* to perform, in the sense of dissimulation. Because criminal fixers withhold his chance at a title bout until he pays for the privilege by throwing a fight, Jake eventually acquiesces and loses to Fox. However, his performance in the charade is so inept or so stubborn or both that it is obvious to all he is not boxing, but pretending, and La Motta is suspended. Joey, his enraged brother-manager, in fact taunts him with play-fighting. He grabs Jake's hand and hits himself with it, and falls to the ground (and half out of the frame) in imitation of a knockdown.

Even while yielding to the fixers, as a "real" boxer and "real man," La Motta has refused to take a literal fall; an oddly similar refusal as that in his third bout with Robinson when he is soundly defeated but numbly taunts his opponent with the fact that he is still standing. In this later fight, Jake's pretense that his verticality is meaningful stands in sharp ironic contrast to his earlier willfully bad imitation of bad boxing, as if bad faith were mitigated by bad acting.

In a sense, it might be asked whether the film's bad faith is miti-gated by its *good* acting. De Niro's performance is justly praised for both its craft and its intensity, and all the hype around his physical transformation for the role is in many ways appropriate, responsible as that effort of an actor's will is for the astonishing change in the filmed character. But whether the "historical" La Motta is a good or bad person, or a good or bad actor, the film narrows its own scope by framing him as a dumb animal. His unknowability, were it not so masculinized and so frequently unattractive, would approach the blank implacability of Cathy Moriarty's brilliant appearance in the film's early scenes. La Motta is a puzzle, not as a great human being, but as an unknowable animal. In some appraisals, in fact, what is "great" about the picture is not that it represents a moment of tragic knowing but depicts instead a person who is broadly unknowing – and fundamentally unknowable. In Janet Maslin's words,

> When Jake point-blank asks his brother to hit him in the face, or when he slams his head against a wall in a Florida jail cell, the film comes its closest to plumbing his depths; it also stands its farthest from reason. We know nothing of Jake's psychology, or his spirituality; even his physical being, constantly changing shape as he gorges himself or diets, is somehow uncertain. When he rails at his wife in a fit of jealousy, his fury is so dissociated from her behavior that the irrational element in his anger is underscored. Any attempt to explain La Motta would surely diminish him. The movie's intense, uncritical embrace of him, by comparison, is its best and only argument for his case. Finally, *it is the generosity of the filmmakers' interest in the La Motta of* Raging Bull *that makes him interesting* [emphasis added].[5]

Largely because La Motta is so obviously not a nice guy, this generosity ultimately redounds to the benefit of the filmmakers, as demonstrated by Maslin's response. The heroism here is not that of the tragic hero, but of the tragic actor – De Niro's heroic act of imagining. Viewed in this way, *Raging Bull* is less a film about a boxer pretending – or not – to be beaten, but about an actor pretending to be that boxer. *Raging Bull* eventually comes to foreground the drama of its own production.

THE ACTOR'S BLUNT INSTRUMENT

The reception of the film has its own dramatic, literally striking, quality. Important among the film's many achievements is that, in the fight scenes, it oscillates between constructing for the audience a relation of kinesthetic identification and of aesthetic objectification. The latter effect is achieved in large part through the combination of evocative sound effects, tight framing, and quick editing; Scorsese in these moments invites us to imagine the experience of being hit. Usually, though not always, it is Jake's experience that is thus framed. This effect alternates with other sequences that distance the spectator from the violence, through changes of angle and slow motion. This dynamic invites viewers first to identify with La Motta (who experiences and dispenses the force which we might imagine feeling) and then with De Niro (the immediately accessible "author" of this beauty). This rhythm may be productively contrasted with the violence performed on De Niro's body at the end of *Taxi Driver* (1976), where Scorsese repeatedly cuts away from the central character Travis, using reaction shots of Jodie Foster to frame even those parts of the gun battle that she doesn't see. In the ending of *Taxi Driver*, De Niro acts himself not into the audience's kinesthetic awareness, as in *Raging Bull*, but into a visually contemplated tableau. In this manner, the violent conclusion of *Taxi Driver* is closer to *Raging Bull*'s final dressing-room scene than to its fight sequences.

If the meta-drama of *Raging Bull* centers around the instrumentality of the actors' bodies and in particular De Niro's body, it is most intense in its attention to the *sharpening* of that instrument in the actor's training with La Motta and its subsequent *blunting* in his celebrated weight gain. Transformation of an actor's body size has remained one of the benchmarks of excellence in cinematic acting, with De Niro's feat often cited as the defining instance of an actor's physical transformation. A recent example, though constructed as self-sacrificing in a different register because of her gender, is Renée Zellwegger's weight gain for the film adaptation of *Bridget Jones' Diary* (2001) and its sequel. Though differently inflected, it is tempting to see in accounts of these performer's processes the projection of a fantasy of absolute physical control. Even the amounts claimed vary widely, averaging around 40 pounds, but with filmmaker Lizzie Borden asserting that she "was completely fascinated by [De Niro's] gaining more than 100 lbs. for his role...De Niro had stepped beyond illusion."[6]

If I am correct that one major entry to the film is identification not with the character of La Motta but with the actor who plays him, then the fascination with De Niro's body is a kind of rupture in the classic formulation of spectatorship of narrative film. Yet, *Raging Bull* can still be understood in a modified version of such a theory of spectatorship. Pam Cook incorporated the actor's body into a feminist psychoanalytic account of the film:

> [F]or those of us turned on by De Niro, the 'real' loss of his beautiful body as an object for contemplation is disturbing, and undermines the sadistic desire to see that body punished and mutilated that

the film activates. The loss of the actor's body, known and desired before the film existed, drawing us to the film with the promise of the pleasure of seeing it, implicates us deeply in the tragic hero's decline. Whatever power we may have thought we had, through our sadistic gaze at the bruised and battered male body, we lose through identification with the hero's loss. The pain of our loss motivates us to look back, to seek again the perfect body in all its power and beauty, as the film itself looks back nostalgically to a time when pure animal energy formed the basis of resistance to opression and exploitation, identifying that energy with masculine virility.[7]

Cook aligns the actor's work with a subversion of the "sadistic" spectatorship that tragedy, in her understanding, invites. Coupled with the way in which the boxing matches are presented, this perhaps means that the film sets up a sado-masochistic dynamic in which spectators can alternately experience both positions.

This possibility, in conjunction with the complications of viewing the film as a drama about actor rather than or as well as character, makes it important to consider the thematics of physicality and violence within the rest of the film's narrative. For example, male potency is doubly valued. Although masculine virility is obsessed over, it is also used as an insult. After the Janiro fight, as he exercises in a steam room trying to make weight, Jake calls his trainer a "fucking hard-on." In the next scene, an enraged Joey calls Salvy the same thing before he beats him up. Beyond simple phallo-phobia, these instances point to the male characters' need to not simply possess masculine power but to control it.

A related image cluster, subtly present at several points, is the pairing of fist and open hand, punch and slap. In one early scene, Jake succeeds in getting Joey to hit him, in part by slapping him three times, while at the same moment insulting his masculinity. Men box men, but slap women. In the montage of boxing matches and color home movies of their domestic life, including their wedding, Vickie and Jake are seen first dancing and then sparring by a swimming pool, mock-slapping at each other (when Jake falls in, he overpowers Vickie and drops her abruptly into the water). Slapping, seen as something for a man to do in play, or to discipline a hysterical or disrespectful woman, is a double insult when done to a man. Later, in between his bouts with Cerdan and Dauthuile, Jake quarrels with Vickie because he suspects her of being involved with Joey. We've seen him slap her, but after breaking down the door of their bathroom to reach her, he draws back his fist and almost punches her, only to then stop himself and leave – to attack his brother. When Vickie catches up with him at Joey's, he does punch her hard with a closed fist, and she falls down, obviously hurt. The characters and the film clearly understand this as a transgression; immediately after, she is packing, threatening to move out.

The differing violences associated with soft and hard, and their attendant sexual connotations, are carried through in another striking pair of images connecting sexual performance with athletic performance. In the interval between his second and third fights with Robinson, Jake appears ready to break his own training regimen with Vickie. "You said never to touch you before a fight," she says, but he tells her to remove her clothes. She begins to kiss his torso, and the implication is that she is about to perform fellatio on him. Jake suddenly breaks away: "I gotta fight Robinson, I can't fool around." Going into the bathroom, he pours a pitcher of ice water down his shorts – a moment that perhaps again catches many spectators out of the narrative and reminds them of the actor's own body.

After the third Robinson fight, which Jake loses, his brother Joey is enraged – we see him smashing a chair against a wall, ranting that Sugar Ray was given the decision because he is going into the military. La Motta's (oft-cited) response is that "I've done a lot of bad things, Joey, maybe it's coming back to me." Dismissing Vickie and the rest of his entourage, Jake sits alone in the dressing room, staring at himself in the mirror (a frequent occurrence in the film). Scorsese first contemplates Jake gazing at himself, then, in a tight close-up, his fist soaking in ice water, which clenches twice, then relaxes, open, sinking slightly into the bucket. Viewers familiar with La Motta's biography might think in this scene of the frequent injuries to his hands that the boxer sustained, but even for those spectators, the scene surely also suggests, beyond the clear connection to his earlier icing of a swollen body part, Jake holding on to and then releasing the rage and power concentrated in his fist.

With this scene of a fight's aftermath, the film includes in its examination of boxing performance the third of the three phases Richard Schechner discerns in all performance: warm-up, event, and "cool down."[8] Two meanings of "performance" are to play and to complete an action. The above images of physical control contrasted with violence are relevant to the film's depiction of performance; they illuminate its two sides, the fictional and the thorough. Slapping is play-fighting, and sex (at least when performed by a woman upon a man) is "fooling around," whereas violence promises finality. It gets the job done. The difficulty for Jake is that he cannot maintain a state of constant violence, the absolute thoroughness of being represented by his actions in the ring. The instrument of violence must relax because without the norm of daily life the extra-daily extremity of performance loses coherence. A related problem for Jake is that daily life itself requires myriad social performances that he cannot master.

PLAYING POSSUM

If La Motta is confused about the relation between action and acting, the production, marketing, and critical discourse around the film often likewise demonstrate conflicting associations with artifice and artistry. These associations double most clearly along gender lines. For example, De Niro portrays a character who seems physically in control only in combat and who cannot reliably manage the self-construction of his image, even when on stage or in the ring. The actor's process in creating this chaotic character, however, was routinely fetishized in the press, most notably his gaining considerable weight to play the older ex-champion in the later scenes. The rest of De Niro's process and technique received considerable attention as well, and published features on the making of the movie clearly cast him as Scorsese's partner in conceptualizing the film, even as they laud a natural and instinctive dimension of his acting.[9]

In contrast, much was made of the "discovery" of Cathy Moriarty, who plays La Motta's second wife, Vickie. Vickie is a mesmerizing and somewhat inscrutable force, who seems to affect Jake almost magically. Two key early scenes establish her power. Jake sees her from a distance at the swimming pool, location of so many of the key encounters showing his connections to the social environment of the Italian-American working-class Bronx neighborhood. Relative to her surroundings, she possesses a Hollywood glamour as she lounges silently, dappled in sunlight reflected from the pool. Later, the film seems to locate Jake's capitulation to her power in their game of mini-golf. Jake helps her make a shot, and Vickie looks under a tiny chapel for her ball, which has disappeared. Time seems briefly to stop as she gazes over her shoulder at Jake. "What does that mean?" she then asks. "It means the game is over," he replies.

A remarkably similar moment later marks the escalation of his violent jealousy. In their hotel suite as they wait for weather to permit the title fight with Cerdan, we see from Jake's point of view a slow-motion shot of Vickie kissing Tommy Como goodbye. Jake slaps her and says to Joey, "I'm disgusted with the two of youse." (In the opening of the next scene, he is brutally punching the sparring pad held by a visibly pained Joey.) In moments like this, Scorsese brings to Jake's passage through daily life the stutter-step pacing that marks the cinematic footwork of the boxing scenes, but this also, albeit very temporarily, positions Vickie in a manner analogous to the fighters he faces in the ring. Her studied blankness (her silence throughout this hotel room sequence is one sullen extreme of it) approximates the otherness of the wild-eyed Sugar Ray as he confronts the camera (representing Jake's point of view) in the third of their fights. The film is sympathetic to her (in contrast to its studied neutrality toward the other fighters) but it nonetheless frames her as to-be-beaten. She must, like Joey and the many speechless opponents Jake boxes, choose between fighting and leaving the game.

Moriarty, unlike De Niro, is seen as an intuitive actor, reliant more on her own being than her willed becoming. As one feature headline has it, "That I Had Never Acted Helped Me to Be Natural."[10] Certainly Moriarty was inexperienced relative to De Niro, and her role in the film is in many ways less complex, yet in the discourse around the film she becomes almost a non-actor, a "natural" in contrast to De Niro's genius. This dynamic becomes clearer if the celebration of Joe Pesci's work is included in a glance at the publicity around the movie. On one level, this representation of the actors' labor is simply more of a typical undervaluing of female creative labor relative to male. This tendency of reception is unwittingly abetted by the film's apparent strategy of representing Jake's incomprehension of the world: Because he doesn't understand Vickie, the film doesn't either. True, Scorsese does contrast Jake's irrational perceptions of her with cooler, more objective shots, but there is no place in this structure for the emotional development that would highlight Moriarty's creative action over her compelling presence. Paradoxically, then, the meta-drama of the film constructs De Niro as a knowing, creative, authorial agent who constructs an unknowing character. La Motta lacks any imagination beyond paranoia and exerts his powerful will on a single dimension. If creative consciousness is seen as constitutive of humanness, then De Niro becomes the more human as his creation, La Motta, becomes more animal.

The boxer's animality – indeed, the animality of the whole social milieu of bloodsport – is highlighted by a number of elements in the film. There are obvious textual references. In the early quarrel between Jake and his first wife, the neighbor calls them animals, and Jake replies, "Who's an animal? Your mother's an animal. You're gonna find your dog dead!" When Joey avers that he never dated Vickie, Jake quips, "She knew you were an animal." After he alleges Joey and Vickie's betrayal, Vickie calls Jake a "sick animal." And Jake wins his 1950 fight against Dauthuile, in the words of the announcer, by "playing possum" before knocking the other fighter out. Finally, of course, Jake confronts, enacts, and denies his animality in his jail cell: "They called me an animal. I'm not an animal . . . I'm not that man."

The visible materiality of the flesh is still more apparent. The boxing sequences are bloody, of course, and punctuated with bone-crunching sound effects. And La Motta worries repeatedly over his physical state, even before his bloated later years. Jake's consumption of flesh is also closely observed. His quarrel with his first wife is over the preparation of a steak. Later, trying to make weight, he's advised to chew a steak up but then spit it out. And the offering Joey makes to Vickie, which so enrages Jake, is a hamburger. The connection of animal and human flesh is driven home in the build-up to the Cerdan fight, when the camera dwells on Jake's corner-men practicing sewing stitches on a steak that a trainer holds above his eye.

Animals, of course, perform in some ways but not in others. In commonsense theories of animal behavior, animals do not "act" as humans do: they don't lie or pretend. Animals do take forceful action, however, in which lies their dangerousness. In a third key sense, however, animals are not seen as performing in the most human of ways, the ways Miller investigates in his thinking through of "Tragedy and the Common Man." Animals are not self-fashioning, or so conventional wisdom has it. They do not will themselves into being; rather, from their animal natures flow their actions. Defined in contrast to animality, then, full humanness is achieved through concerted, conscious acts of self-production.

From the film's title, its language, its physical palpability (literally, as in the shots of a trainer's hands massaging Jake's blood-sponged abdomen), and even the animal cries audible in the soundtrack, *Raging Bull* emphasizes the animality of its protagonist and thus the humanness of its director and lead actor. This process reaches its zenith in the appearance of the fatted bull representing the sacrificial commitment of De Niro's beauty. In turn, this ultimate image of the animal pivots on a question of performance: whether the boxer moves beyond performing tricks, in the manner of a trained animal, and fully contends with the world around him.

ENDING BETWEEN PRETENDING AND CONTENDING

The end of *Raging Bull* appears to bookend the opening boxing sequence but to invert its aesthetics. At the Barbazon Plaza, alone in his dressing room except for a brief interruption as he is cued by a stage hand (an almost invisible cameo by Scorsese), La Motta prepares for a cultural performance rather than an athletic one. He runs through his act facing the mirror, an apparent continuation of the brief backstage scene that follows the beginning titles. But where the opening is distant, aestheticized, and lifted out of time, the conclusion is a close-up as brutal in its own way as the boxing shots. De Niro is puffy, his face a pocked and pasty mess, his act clearly something of an embarrassment. Or is it?

The bit he's rehearsing, Marlon Brando's "I could have been a contender" speech from *On the Waterfront*, has long been associated with good acting, though that association comes in part from *Raging Bull* itself. Indeed, Budd Schulberg's celebrated lines in Elia Kazan's film are, if anything, a rather understated moment of confrontation between Brando's character, Terry Malloy, and his brother Charlie, played by Rod Steiger. Although they prompt a change of conscience in their addressee, the drama of the moment is subtle rather than blatant. The lines are perhaps often misremembered as a climactic, anguished plea for understanding, but in the scene with Brando and Steiger, the effect, even though Terry's life hangs in the balance, is of recognition, resignation, and matter-of-fact explanation. Brando seems almost exasperated with his brother, and it might even be argued that Charlie's subsequent reversal seems unmotivated.

Still, Brando's subtlety aside, De Niro's representation of La Motta's rehearsal hardly celebrates Jake's own acting ability. His memorization is rote, flat of affect, and his failure of interpretation seems to state bluntly that there is no tragic recognition here. The ostensible meaning of the passage is that La Motta is in show business, even at its margins, only by virtue of his own notoriety, and that he does not realize that himself, although he may believe his delivery of the speech has meaning. For Gail and Thomas Hemmeter, it appears that "they have only ironic significance" – that the citation of a filmic passage about insight here signifies its opposite.[11]

If this is the gist of the monologue as De Niro rehearses it in the film, La Motta, perhaps not surprisingly, has disagreed, albeit in terms that undermine his defense. In 2001, for example, he insisted: "I did that. I did it word perfect I can guarantee you. . . . That was a great movie, great lines. 'I could've been a contender. I could've had class and been somebody. Instead of a bum, let's face it, which is what I am.' I knew Budd back then, he was a great writer."[12]

The interpretation of this passage of La Motta's life has not been his to control, however, and the common reading of his life, summed up in Jack Kroll's phrase – "the gladiator fading into show business"[13] – offers a satisfying coherence to the film. A powerful fighter becomes a forceless performer. But the story isn't over. One element within the film's ending challenges this account of the central character, while subsequent re-tellings of the ending challenge this standard interpretation.

In 1997, HBO Boxing produced a promotional advertisement for its televised fights featuring the aging Jake La Motta. In a boxing ring, shot in black and white, his white hair part of a broad, smoky back-lit halo, the boxer recites the same speech from *On the Waterfront*. This version of the speech could be understood as trying to graft the aesthetics of *Raging Bull*'s opening shot to the interest in character demonstrated by its ending. La Motta looks old and heavy, but the view is soft-focus. Instead of a single, rather excruciating lingering shot, the commercial cuts between angles and interposes atmospheric shots of the boxing club. And rather than the noticeably empty silence between De Niro's phrases, the ad invokes the classical score of so much of the rest of the film (though in this case with a choral background). Most importantly, La Motta *looks like he understands what he's saying.* Indeed, for this production, the pathos is predicated on that self-awareness, as La Motta ends the speech with visible regret on the line "I coulda been a contender, instead of a bum, which is what I am." The television piece thus constructs La Motta as an actor of at least basic competence, as well as a man aware of the lowered status that represents relative to being champ. This much of the promo enacts a task that performance theorist Patrice Pavis assigns to performance analysis, that it should consider "other options for possible mise-en-scenes."[14] In other words, in its invocation or refunctioning of elements of *Raging Bull*'s construction, the commercial reads across the fine grain of the earlier depiction of La Motta. The pathos of the moment highlights the extent to which the end of *Raging Bull* depends on a kind of animal blankness in De Niro's fat face. The commercial clarifies that Maslin's appreciation of the filmmakers' "generosity" is, in a sense, the interpretation the movie asks for. In this last scene, La Motta is every bit as present as he is in the rest of the film, but he is overshadowed by the *act* of movie-making. Scorsese arrives for his cameo as De Niro rehearses the antithesis of an Oscar acceptance speech.

Of course, the sentimental HBO advertisement has a further twist on *Raging Bull*'s apparent foreclosure of self-knowledge on the boxer's part. The conclusion of his monologue is punctuated by applause from a group of young, handsome boxers gathered around La Motta in the ring, and he offers a small crafty smile, as if to suggest that his stubborn persistence has in fact won him wisdom and a measure of redemption, at least by late twentieth-century media-culture terms. It suggests not only that La Motta can offer a dramatically functional recitation of the monologue, but that he is savvy about the circumstances in which he performs it, that he consciously manipulates his audiences' understanding of his performance process. In *Raging Bull*, Scorsese makes La Motta into a petty brute of mythic stature as personified by De Niro; in the cable boxing advertisement, HBO both humanizes him and makes the aging boxer into a little De Niro, with his own modicum of craft and sly self-promotion.

Had *Raging Bull* ended with the *On the Waterfront* speech, these two cinematic representations of La Motta as either baffled animal or avuncular survivor would be available in pristine opposition. And the film might be open to an admittedly unsophisticated critique of its biographical ethics. But the movie has perhaps had Jake playing possum. Scorsese works to complete the link back to its opening sequence, and La Motta rises from his dressing room mirror and shadow-boxes before heading to the stage. He pumps his arms, breathing hard, and rapidly repeats "I'm the boss, I'm the boss, I'm the boss." De Niro repeats this three times, but with an improvisational quality rather than a feeling of structuring a climax. *Raging Bull* almost condemns the cinematic La Motta to an eternity of bad acting, but in this final gesture, perhaps seeks to place him in the limbo of an *ongoing* performance. It at least allows the opportunity to judge La Motta's performances not in terms of points scored and thus fights won or lost, and not on the terms of screen acting. The end of the film almost asks for a consideration of La Motta derived from now commonplace critical considerations of some contemporary performance art and popular performance. In such cases, the issue is not whether the work is effectively mimetic, but whether it is *committed*.

Such a reading requires a comparison of La Motta not to Brando but to endurance body artists, both those credentialed in art world performance and many not. For example, Chris Burden's performances in the 1970s involved bodily mortifications, including living confined to an art school locker, having himself shot in the arm, and being briefly "crucified" on a Volkswagen. The Australian artist Stelarc continues to create performances, such as his "suspensions" in which he was hung from hooks, recent work in which his muscles have been wired to machines and even the Internet, and numerous other ways in which he has given his body (which he consistently refers to in the third person as "the body") over to art. These artists represent a field of performance work that is very diverse, yet notable for the creation of a sense of white masculinity constituted through stoic suffering. In recent popular culture, the magician David Blain has gained renown through Houdini-esque stunts, such as being encased in ice, buried alive, and suspended in a transparent box without food for several weeks.

Clearly, there is great distance between such performances and the work of film actors, but the key terms in appreciating such work for many have been endurance and persistence, qualities that can be found both in De Niro's sacrificial acting and in La Motta's dogged performance career. On such perhaps anachronistic terms, La Motta's life performance might even be seen to be judged by the film as successful. The operative comparison would be not to Brando's performance of Terry's speech, but to Terry's actions in the film. La Motta's insistence on continuing to perform is more like Terry's walk to the dock at the end of *On The Waterfront*; having been "a bum," he *goes on* to struggle with something, anything. Of course, read this way, the film would remain subject to the same critiques of macho posturing and nostalgia for masculine potency – these have been productively applied to male body artists as well. But this strategy does allow *Raging Bull* to be seen not as yielding to its latent cultural elitism but as perhaps more ambivalently charting the efforts of a protagonist who continues to contend.

"I'D RATHER RECITE..." OR, WHY ACTING (MASCULINE) IS BETTER THAN FIGHTING

Although they arguably do not alter the structure of the film "itself," even more recent rehearsals of the raging bull character indicate the degree to which this imagery has been culturally *productive* beyond its apparent end. Two brief examples will in fact suggest that *Raging Bull* continues to be re-read in ways that complicate and deepen that depiction of masculinity even as they rely on it.

Judith Halberstam's influential *Female Masculinity* explores numerous performances of masculinity by women, including both "pre-twentieth-century genders," filmic representations, and the performances of drag kings in contemporary clubs. A foundational contention of her study is that "masculinity does not belong to men."[15] The cover of Halberstam's book reproduces a portrait painted by Sadie Lee, titled *Raging Bull*, which the author discusses in her concluding chapter, titled "Raging Bull (Dyke)." The masculine woman in the painting has a "butch gaze," Halberstam writes. "This look, the look of a raging bull, the stare down, the challenge, lets the viewer know that this is the stage where this bull can rage, and though she can fight...she'd rather recite. That's entertainment."[16]

This authorial re-performance of De Niro's performance (of La Motta's shtick) caps the book's final critical reading, a brief analysis of *Raging Bull* itself. Unlike the numerous films Halberstam examines for their representations of women, *Raging Bull* is analyzed here for the construction of masculinity on a male body. *Raging Bull* is rare because it "really take[s] apart male masculinity in a way that allows us to see both its structure and its weaknesses." Her appreciation and appropriation of the figure of La Motta is strong evidence that, in spectatorship as in performance, masculinity does not belong to men. Halberstam sums up the ending with a version of the interpretation that stops short of the film's trajectory – that "the raging bull has been reduced to insipid rhymes."[17] However, her rewriting of Jake's nightclub act as her authorial sign-off reflects a cinematic as well as a critical accomplishment.

If Halberstam constructs an identification with the raging bull in conjunction with her reading of the film's depiction of the aging La Motta as abject, another almost contemporaneous cinematic homage to Scorsese's last scene, Paul Thomas Anderson's *Boogie Nights* (1997), borrows that air of perhaps futile and pitiable pomposity. A similarly open-ended conclusion marks this film about another sphere of male masculine performance – pornography. In the final scene, Mark Wahlberg, as the excessively endowed porn star Dirk Diggler, sits in his dressing room, rehearsing his lines in front of a mirror. The framing and dialogue clearly invoke *Raging Bull*, but he flatly delivers a speech about the depth of penetration he is about to impose on his co-star. He exits the scene in a manner strongly reminiscent of De Niro's shadow-boxing "I'm the boss." But whereas Jake monologues about dreaming he has forgotten to wear shorts into the ring, Dirk knows that nakedness is his business, and he first poses to reassure himself. In the mirror, we see him open his fly and remove his enormous penis, which hangs limply down the front of his pants. "You're a star," he repeats.

As I have implied, I think Anderson references *Raging Bull* both as an homage and to borrow its sense of futility and folly. Dirk is

comical for treating porn acting with an aesthetic pretension even beyond La Motta's attitude toward his act. In De Niro's role, the scene's
visual quality is set by the harsh light on his puffy face and distended
belly; Wahlberg's prosthetic penis has a comparable pasty improba-
bility about it. And like Halberstam's critical sparring, that blunt instrument might also retrospectively alter the meaning of the earlier
film, as Wahlberg's excess flesh de-naturalizes De Niro's. Both films
mock their protagonists for vanity and hubris, but both also imply
a perseverance that exceeds fleshy decay. Although it is not tenable
to propose a mode of performance that is somehow free from the
historical fact of La Motta's male body, Halberstam's and Wahlberg's
re-citations suggest this: Rather than a *failure* at managing his masculinity, the Jake of the final scene of *Raging Bull* has found an arena –
self-consciously theatrical performance – in which he achieves masculine *success*. At the least, his display of masculinity mimes power
rather than abusing it. At this low point of his supposed degradation,
the washed-up boxer is laughable, but that means he is much less to
be feared. And instead of beating either men or women with his fists,
he shadow-boxes for his own satisfaction. Imitation, even if parodic,
and even of one's self, is still a form of flattery.

NOTES

1. Pam Cook, "Masculinity in Crisis? Scorsese's *Raging Bull*," *Screen* 23, no. 3–4 (1982): 40.
2. Judith Halberstam, *Female Masculinity* (Durham: Duke University Press, 1998), 274.
3. Arthur Miller, "Tragedy and the Common Man," in *The Theater Essays of Arthur Miller* (New York: Viking, 1978), 3–7.
4. Fred Ferretti, "The Delicate Art of Creating a Brutal Fight Film," *New York Times*, 23 November 1980, sec. 2: 1.
5. Janet Maslin, "When Puzzles Become Provocative," *New York Times*, 8 February 1981, sec. 2: 21.
6. Lizzie Borden, "Blood and Redemption," *Sight and Sound* n.s. 5 (February 1995): 61.
7. Cook, "Masculinity in Crisis?" 42–43.
8. This is discussed in several of Schechner's works. A clear summary of this stand of his scholarship is found in Richard Schechner, *Performance Studies: An Introduction* (New York: Routledge, 2002).
9. See, for example, Ferretti, "Delicate Art."

10. Judy Klemesrud, "That I Had Never Acted Helped Me to Be Natural," *New York Times*, 15 November 1980, sec. 1: 13.

11. Gail Carnicelli Hemmeter and Thomas Hemmeter, "The Word Made Flesh: Language in *Raging Bull*," *Literature / Film Quarterly* 14, no. 2 (1986): 104.

12. Steve Bunce, "*Raging Bull* Was Released 20 Years Ago This Month," *Scotland on Sunday*, 25 November 2001: 33.

13. Jack Kroll, "De Niro's 'Bronx Bull,'" *Newsweek*, 24 November 1980, 128.

14. Patrice Pavis, *Analyzing Performance: Theatre, Dance and Film*, trans. David Williams (Ann Arbor: University of Michigan Press, 2003), 39.

15. Halberstam, *Female Masculinity*, 241.

16. Halberstam, *Female Masculinity*, 277.

17. Halberstam, *Female Masculinity*, 275.

4 Women in *Raging Bull*

Scorsese's Use of Determinist, Objective, and Subjective Techniques

In *Raging Bull*, Martin Scorsese uses a variety of techniques to control access to his characters, particularly his female characters. The limitations upon the range and depth of knowledge into the characters reveal his debt to literary naturalism and Italian Neorealism. In both literary and cinematic representations of naturalist reality, characters are often portrayed objectively: They are known primarily through dialogue and action. Even when they are portrayed subjectively, the audience remains aware of their limited knowledge of the overall circumstances in which they function. Naturalist authors and directors use such limitations to simulate the forms of determinism that circumscribe humans' range of options, the social, economic, historical, psychological, and physical forces controlling our actions. This extreme authorial control of characters' lives represents the iron grip that its proponents believe controls our own lives.

Such determinist ideology shapes *Raging Bull* in general and especially in regard to women characters. They cannot be studied as subjects of the film text, for they have no subjective viewpoints of their lives. Further, there is no omniscient narrative insight into their feelings about their lives. Women must, then, be studied in relation to Jake's perspective because they are only known in the film as constructs of Jake's subjectivity once they become objects of interest to him. There are three types of women in *Raging Bull*, which roughly correspond to the film's structure. Irma (Lori Anne Flax), Jake's first wife, has two scenes only. Cathy Moriarty as Vickie La Motta, Jake's second wife, has numerous scenes throughout Acts 1 and 2 but disappears from Act 3 when she leaves him after eleven years of abuse. In Act 3, only barmaids, exotic dancers, or wives of patrons are presented not just briefly but anonymously in Jake's club or in other nightclubs in which he performs his recitations. The film presents these women's consciousness in one of three ways: as uninteresting to know; as unknown; or, worst of all, in Vickie's case, unknowable and therefore an object of obsessive, frustrated, violently jealous scrutiny on Jake's part. I have extrapolated this know-ability context with which I am examining females in the film from suggestions made by Laura Mulvey in "Visual Pleasure and Narrative Cinema." Mulvey's study from the early 1970s, now a classic analysis of narrative control of women's power in film, provides a useful theoretical context in which to examine the narrative determinism affecting all characters, but particularly women in *Raging Bull*.[1]

These three categories of women are known only as objects of Jake's interest. The film's naturalist worldview defines Jake as the narrative's focus. La Motta, as constructed in the screenplay of Paul Schrader and Mardik Martin, reflects historical, cultural, social, economic, physical, and psychological gender ideologies. Jake is the product of his childhood during the worst part of America's Great Depression. His background as an Italian-American child of immigrants shapes his identity; his native Bronx provides the setting in which poverty and his Italian-American culture permanently affected him; and finally, his own genetic accidents of physical toughness, violent temper, and ambition factor into his expectations of male and female behavior. Jake emerges from the film as a deeply insecure, violently tempered, sexually paranoid, profoundly ambitious, extremely traditionalist male who, in the 1940s and 1950s, brawls his way to the middleweight championship.

It is intriguing to examine how Scorsese rivets audience interest in Jake's brutality to everyone, women and himself included. The narration's control of what we know and how we know it creates much of our interest in Jake. First, as the center of the frame story and internal flashback, there is almost no action at which Jake is not just present but the center of the camera's attention. In the four sequences with Joey, although Jake is not actually on screen, he remains very much the subject of the action. Second, Scorsese gives La Motta multiple access to the audience, not only as the subject of the two objective temporal narratives but also as the perceiver of sequences shot as deep inside perceptual subjective points of view. These subjective point-of-view sequences, in both the matches and Jake's domestic life with Vickie, function as movies within movies, with their own cinematography and soundtracks to create for the audience an intimate experience of how it looks and feels to be Jake.

Such multiplying and stylizing of Jake's interior experiences goes far to make us identify with him, despite his behavior. These multiplied objective and subjective points of view for Jake constitute filmic equivalents of Wayne Booth's deep inside views of protagonists. Scorsese's varied cinematographic representations of Jake's experience yield the same deep identification of audience with protagonist that Booth identified as the consequence of such a technique. As Booth notes about late-nineteenth century experiments in deep inside point of view with non-traditional protagonists such as Dostoevsky's Raskolnikov, the deeper our knowledge of such characters, however unlikable, the more likely we are to accept and even sympathize with them.[2] Third, the film as constructed text constitutes Aristotelian spectacle, from which we cannot turn our eyes, as it shows us how it looks and feels to dispense and receive physical brutality.[3] In this respect, Scorsese's violence functions as does violence to the human body in horror films – as a magnet, toward which we are drawn without wanting to be, compelled to watch.[4]

In contrast, women remain objects of the camera's eye. They are scripted as the constructs of both the objective narrative and Jake's subjective points of view. In the former, Scorsese presents women in subsidiary roles within Jake's story – as wives, girlfriends, and mother to his children. The film limits access to women; they are known through their actions, dialogue, and Jake's dialogue about women. Consistent with his upbringing, Jake objectifies women along the lines of the two resolutions possible for women Mulvey identifies as either good girls or bad girls. Mulvey argues that Classic Hollywood cinema represents women in extremely limited stereotypical roles – virgin, wife and mother, or villain and whore – and reiterates the Victorian stereotypes from which these narrowly defined roles historically descend. Both sexually-safe women and those who are not end up reduced through narrative closure to similar fates: They are objectified, anatomized, and fetishized. Because men, not women,

remain the center of Classic Hollywood narration, the chief difference between good and bad women lies not in what they become by
the conclusion of the picture but rather how soon they are placed
into one of these culturally acceptable categories. Good women are
immediately limited in their behavior and psychological development to remain morally safe; thus, their narrative trajectory is pre-
dictable. Good women can go bad, but then they suffer the same end
as women who appear from the outset of the narrative to be sexually
suspect. Bad girls are punished and therefore also made safe for the
respectable, Breen-Code ending required for loose women.

Both good and bad women are, in addition to being controlled by
the narration's prescribed outcomes for them, also controlled cin-
ematographically. Mulvey points out that women are photograph-
ically anatomized – emphasizing particular parts of the woman's
body, such as Marlene Dietrich's face lit to emphasize her cheek-
bones or shots of Betty Grable showcasing her legs. According to
Mulvey's psychoanalytic argument, anatomization diminishes a cas-
tration anxiety generated by full-body photography of the woman
in the film's narrative. She is reduced to only a part of herself, an
image safer to the male audience projected by Classic Hollywood
cinema. Such anatomized, fetishistic cinematography is the creation
of the male-dominated film industry during the 1940s and 1950s.
A sexually desirable (and therefore threatening) woman on screen
is reduced to a man-made fetish, a two-dimensional icon. Dietrich,
in repeated bad-girl roles, becomes Von Sternberg's enactment of his
Dietrich creation, portraying his version of beautiful female product
crafted for the camera's eye, the voyeuristic male audience projected
by such cinematography. Such product crafting out of the female
body renders the sexually attractive woman as unreal. Essentially an
embodiment of male fantasy, she is a producible commodity of the
Hollywood film industry, endlessly re-packaged in newer, younger
versions of this iconic female.

IRMA: THE SHRIKE

In *Raging Bull*, Irma La Motta, Jake's first wife, is intriguingly represented relative to Mulvey's theory. She has only two very brief scenes
at the film's beginning. No one uses her first name within the movie;

in the final credits, she is identified only as Irma, not Irma La Motta. Within the overall narration, she disappears upon cue, after Jake spots, falls for, and takes up with Vickie. Most significantly, in her two scenes, I cannot discern Scorsese utilizing any element of film technique to create sympathy for her abandoned, first-wife character. Rather, she is only characterized – in costume, dialogue, line delivery, and body movements – as a shrike. Graphically, narratively, temporally, and spatially, she seems to be presented as unflatteringly as possible. Lori Anne Flax as Irma is physically the opposite of Vickie: with brown hair, brown eyes, and olive complexion. In both scenes, she is costumed in housecoats, a 1930s or 1940s working-class wives' dress for kitchen, house, and child-rearing duties. She wears her long hair in a distinctively 1940s style featuring hair parted down the middle and rolled up on both sides, a style Joan Crawford wears to great effect in *Mildred Pierce* (1945). Her nondescript appearance implicitly contrasts with Vickie's more updated, Lana Turneresque platinum blonde hair, teenage appearance (although extremely physically mature), and highly stylized costumes.

Irma's first scene begins, as do almost all scenes in the film, with the camera on Jake, center frame. He is in an undershirt and boxers that reveal De Niro's remarkable physical conditioning to portray the younger Jake. He sits at the kitchen table; his first line is "They know who's the boss," a dialogue motif for Jake that Scorsese repeats as the last lines of the movie. The line becomes a mantra that Jake repeats to himself before going on stage. Here in his own kitchen in 1941, he's referring to his fight with Jimmy Reeves the previous night, in which the judges awarded the match to Reeves. The unruly audience was so much in favor of Jake that a brawl broke out among the crowd signifying their adamant disagreement with the decision. Jake, upon Joey's advice as his manager, refuses to leave the ring as they recognize the crowd's preference for Jake. In the kitchen, Jake adds that "the judges know who won; the people knew who won," to congratulate himself in the face of his first professional loss.

Having asserted himself, he then segues into criticism of the unnamed Irma, although their character proxemics clearly identify who she is: "You thought I was over there foolin' around; I wasn't foolin' around. That's in your mind!" The last line will connect in terms of psychological causation when Jake adopts this suspicious mindset toward Vickie, suggesting that infidelity is a pervasive element in their culture, behavior that is true once he becomes involved with Vickie while still married to Irma. Since he cheated on Irma, he seems to bring that suspicion to his relations with Vickie in an escalated form because of Vickie's highly sexualized appearance. Irma's first line, in response to Jake's charge of her unwarranted suspicions that previous night, is a belligerently delivered response: "Yeah, so what?" In the face of his subsequent infidelity with Vickie, Irma's unwillingness here to acknowledge that she was wrong about the previous evening suggests non-diegetic story elements that justify her angry suspicion of Jake. He continues his corrective criticism by adding, "That championship belt" – used throughout the film as a visual motif measuring Jake's career ups and downs – "that's why I'm foolin' around." He thus redefines "foolin' around" as fighting in his rejoinder – placing him through dialogue, along with his (relatively mild for Jake) line delivery up to this point in the film, as focused solely upon winning the middleweight championship.

Jake, plate and utensils before him at the table, asks Irma if the steak she is cooking is done and admonishes her, "Don't overcook it. You overcook it, it defeats its own purpose." Irma, in reverse shot, says, "No," and her body language and appearance as she stands before the stove express bitterness. She glares angrily back at Jake in silence. Scorsese conveys volumes about the couple's clearly habitual anger toward one another in these two scenes. The camera returns to Jake, who ratchets up the hostility by demanding, "What are ya doin'? Don't overcook it. I just said don't overcook it. Bring it over here." When she doesn't immediately respond to his order, he yells at her, "Bring it over here; it's like a piece of charcoal," though from his position at the kitchen table, he is unable to see the steak.

Scorsese, in returning to the reverse shot of Irma, pulls the camera back just far enough so that we can see that the kitchen is built with a partial wall between the stove and the table. That partial wall has a window without glass in it, so the cook can hand food to family at the table. Here, the opening creates a literal frame in which Irma at the stove is boxed. Thus framed, she is a picture of furious but as of yet unexpressed anger: "You want your steak; you want your steak?" She finally explodes, marching from stove to table with skillet in hand. She spears the very large steak; it dangles precariously from the end of the fork before she slaps it onto his plate. Shouting, she repeats a third time, "You want your steak," while spooning a mountain of potatoes onto Jake's plate. In response to his no longer aggressive response of "That's all I want," she retorts, "No, more!" Jake, compelled to crush any aggression mounted toward him, jerks to his feet, deliberately throwing the table and its contents down to the floor. "You bothering me about a steak?" he inquires twice, ready to respond physically to her audacity in not complying quietly with his demands. Both actors are in full-frame shots. He is moving into the kitchen toward her; she is trying to move away from him. She is still shouting – albeit with desperation, not anger now – "I'm so sick of you" while stamping her foot in impotent, childlike frustration.

Scorsese cuts to the building's exterior, where Joey is agreeing with Salvy (Frank Vincent) to talk to Jake again about accepting the patronage of the local mob boss, Tommy Como (Nicholas Colasanto). This conversation introduces another narrative element that valorizes La Motta. He wants to avoid mob ties and make it on his own to middleweight champion, an impossibility, given boxing's ties to the mob during the 1940s and 1950s. Scorsese later re-emphasizes this valorization of Jake's independence when he finally agrees to mob support to get access to a title shot. After he takes a mob-required dive in a match with Billy Fox, Scorsese photographs Jake – the quintessential stoic American male – crying, heartbroken in the arms of his trainer. The trainer, also moved to tears in response to Jake, exclaims "Quit fighting; quit fighting." Like a Greek chorus, the trainer expresses what the sequence as staged wants us to feel: how wrong it is that honest boxers like Jake have no chance on their own to win championship because the boxing industry is so corrupt. Here, as Joey enters Jake's apartment building, his last words to Salvy, a mobster with whom Joey is friends but Jake despises, are "If he's in a good mood, I'll bring it [working for Tommy] up to him." On the aural periphery of the soundtrack while Joey and Salvy talk, Scorsese ironically overlaps the faintly detectable noise of the couple screaming at each other upstairs.

Walking into the apartment, Joey registers no surprise at the argument, giving us another cue that the couple's fighting is habitual. Measuring volubility only, in both scenes, while Jake argues with Irma, she screams louder than Jake. This serves several rhetorical purposes: first, she becomes the most unpleasant aggressive sound in the movie thus far. Anyone who has endured Marilyn Burns' screaming throughout *The Texas Chainsaw Massacre* (1974) knows how unpleasant women's screams can be made to register on a film's soundtrack. Compared with Irma's yelling, Jake's pitch is lower not just because De Niro's voice is lower but also because De Niro is playing Jake here as upset yet still in charge of the argument's trajectory. He raises his voice only as much as he needs to. Later scenes of domestic violence with Vickie will show far greater escalation of Jake's temper. Jake's line to Irma as he marches into the kitchen expresses his complete conviction that she is responsible for the argument. In response to her complaints about what he's done to the food she's cooked and the table, he declares "I got no choice; I got no choice," in that Bronx-accented cadence that De Niro delivers perfectly.

Once Joey comes into the apartment, Jake loses interest in the fight, preferring his brother's company to Irma's. He makes short work of their dispute by grabbing Irma by the back of her hair and marching her toward, then just shoving her into, their bedroom. The net effect is his physical imposition of a disciplinarian's "Time Out" upon Irma, who knows from experience to close herself inside their bedroom doors, where she is still yelling and kicking objects in the room. Seemingly as an offhand remark, Jake shouts twice to Irma, "You break anything in there, I swear I'll kill ya." We hear her muffled response, "Yeah, sure." Scorsese focuses our attention on a medium two shot of Jake and Joey at the table. To signal the beginning of their conversation, Scorsese initially has Jake turned away from Joey toward the bedroom. When Jake turns back to Joey, De Niro shows us his rare, very appealing smile. He jokes to Joey about Irma while laughing, "What's she doin?" to convey his mystification about the dust-up that, in his mind, Irma created. He closes the argument by saying to Irma, who is still inside the closed bedroom doors, "Come on, honey; let's not fight. Truce?" While Irma volubly grumbles from the bedroom, Jake is perfectly calm, ready to converse with Joey.

This dispute establishes the pattern of Jake's domestic arguments that never changes, except in degree of violence, throughout the film. He begins or rather lives in a perennially volatile mood. In this state of angry explosion about to happen, Jake has a "hair trigger" temper that flares up at anyone who behaves toward him as if he were not "the boss."[5] As he loses his temper, he first interrogates his target according to his paranoid construction of reality. An imagined slight or lack of respect toward him elicits increasingly pointed, often maddeningly repeated questions to the object of his scrutiny, as in his repeated insistence that Irma overcooked his steak. When his questions are not met with the answers his agitated psyche needs, he explodes into physical violence. In contrast to the close-up photography of Jake's violence in the ring, Scorsese typically shoots Jake's domestic violence at a greater distance in relatively short takes. Nonetheless, La Motta's physical abuse toward those closest to him is a wrenching experience to witness. Here, Scorsese achieves a rhetorical affect upon the audience analogous to the bruising action represented within the film. Violence within and outside of the ring is relentlessly paced, a key factor in the film's exhausting effect upon audiences. Finally, it's a key element to Jake's rage pattern that, after his outbursts, De Niro as Jake is as sweet-tempered as he ever gets. He either has no memory of the fight in which he just participated, as in this scene with Irma, or he is sincerely remorseful, pleading to patch relations up, as we see later with Vickie.

In this introduction to Irma, Scorsese has been singularly unflattering to her character, given his portrayal of her sullen, bitter, screeching, foot-stamping presence. It's a relief to us when Jake puts her in the bedroom. She has a second final scene, which is an escalated version of the first in terms of her termagant, shrewish behavior. We've known nothing of her consciousness, her reasons for her sullenness. There is nothing narratively, pictorially, or in character development that interests us in her. She appears of no interest to the camera except for Scorsese's character and narrative opportunities that give us our first inside look into Jake's home. Her negative characterization, the lack of any visual or aural element used to represent her as worth our attention in the objective narration, and the lack of any subjective point of view for Irma in her two scenes skews sympathy toward Jake when he subsequently courts the fifteen-year-old Vickie as if he were single.

The screenplay implicitly, thus, justifies Jake's philandering through Irma's tiring bitchiness viewed only objectively and from a completely restricted consciousness. The objective narration characterizes Irma as immediately known and clearly uninteresting. Although Jake is volatile, he has also been physically courageous and

16. "A Lana Turnerish blonde with the sultry, sun-baked appeal of the 1940s *Life* magazine cover."

fiercely determined in the ring, as well as independent of the mob. Irma has none of our interest or sympathy, whereas Jake has both at this point in Act 1, when he spots Vickie at the neighborhood swimming pool and is fascinated by her difference from Irma and all other women in his neighborhood.

VICKIE: THE TROPHY WIFE

Scorsese shoots Jake's first look at Vickie, at the neighborhood swimming pool, with unadulterated scopophiliac pleasure (Figure 16). In shooting a neo-Neorealist biographical film set in the 1940s, Scorsese deliberately shoots Vickie in the sexually objectified manner of the Classic Hollywood cinema that engendered Mulvey's analysis. Scorsese both reveals and revels in film theory's historical awareness of the sexual and economic consequences of such photography of women. This first Vickie sequence begins on Jake center frame. He is at the concession stand gruffly ordering a Coke, in a mid close-up shot, with his back to the camera but with his head turned at a ninety-degree angle to the right, looking intently at an unseen object off screen. That object, and I use the term here deliberately to indicate Scorsese's photography of Cathy Moriarty as a standout platinum blonde, is beautiful by any standards but particularly notable in this working-class 1941 Bronx neighborhood. She is clearly the best-looking girl in Jake's neighborhood, a fifteen-year-old trophy girl who is voluptuous yet girlishly sweet, so physically well endowed and so artificially made up to be attractive according to cultural standards for women at the time that she could pass for twenty-five.

The reverse shot sequence demonstrates all this about Vickie. The sequence also reveals that she is sitting with Salvy and his cronies. Jake grills Joey about Vickie. He has to know if she's from "the neighborhood," how well she knows Salvy because she is sitting with him, and whether Salvy or Joey "ever fucked" her. His immediate need to know about her in order to know if he should know her more intimately demonstrates Mulvey's point that, as soon as the audience – and we are confined to Jake's perspective of Vickie in this as in most scenes – sees Vickie, we, like Jake, feel her desirability. His interrogation of Joey initiates the psychological and verbal motif that dominates Jake's every action toward Vickie from the moment he sees her and, in seeing, becomes covetous of her sexuality as his sole possession. Jake confers upon Vickie her cultural status as valuable sexual fetish when he asks her on their first date "Do you know how beautiful you are?" He answers his question himself: "Yeah, you do. People tell you all the time how beautiful you are." Jake is uninterested in her answer, her subjective experience of how it feels to look as she does; rather, he is concerned only with his neighborhood culture's identification of her trophied status.

From this moment, Jake becomes the prisoner of his desire for and his fear of Vickie; all of his actions toward her can be read through this psychological filter. When he thinks he owns her sexual behavior, he feels empowered. If he fears that this is not true, he becomes a madman, repeatedly attacking Vickie and Joey verbally and physically. Scorsese's film subjects Vickie to both of the fates Mulvey outlines for sexually attractive women in Classic Hollywood cinema. First, Jake fetishizes Vickie as a beautiful platinum blonde with a movie star's face. Second, he repeatedly punishes her for creating his anxiety over his ownership of her sexuality. As represented in the film, Vickie's entire life with Jake alternates between her experience of his desire, tenderness, and economic purchase of her favors and his abuse of her when he is gripped by his obsessive fear that she has been unfaithful.

Vickie is thus initially and repeatedly surveilled, investigated, and dominated by Jake's gaze. Schrader, Martin, and Scorsese construct Jake's experience of the world without Jake's or our understanding of how women in relationships with him felt when they were intimate with this powerful, complex, volatile man. The film creates three separate visual representations of Jake's experience with Vickie: the objective narration, the "home movies" of their early years, and Jake's moments of perceptual subjectivity, surveilling Vickie. Each style portrays another facet of how life looked and felt to him. Examining the women in each film style deepens our understanding of Jake and also represents how women looked, spoke to, and behaved with him. These film styles do not convey how she felt as the object of his attention. In the objective narration, Jake chooses Vickie for his trophy girl and second wife; as such, she functions as a responder to Jake's behavior.

The home movie sequences allow Scorsese a second visual medium within the film to express Jake's way of looking at the world. These movies are stylistically extremely conventional in their late 1940s–early 1950s suburban composition of the courtship, wedding, and early years of marriage of "the perfect couple." Initially, Vickie agreeably exhibits herself as his sexual trophy as in the two swimming pool sequences, one in which she wears a white two-piece bathing suit complete with Lana-Turner-Postman-Rings-Twice turban and a second in which she wears a black two-piece swimming suit. The courtship is followed by their wedding ceremony as well as Joey's wedding, then Jake carrying Vickie over the threshold of their first home, followed by scenes at their suburban home, such as Jake barbecuing in a "Mother's Little Helper" apron, and finally Vickie and Lenore – Joey's wife – with their children in their yards.

These home movie sequences show the couple's stereotypical fantasy of their domestic life in poignant contrast to the explosive "reality" of their lives in the objective narration. In the color home movies, Vickie appears to make the transition successfully from Jake's sexual trophy to the bearer of his name and the mother of his children. Scorsese shoots these home movies so conventionally that their marked contrast to the objective narration suggests that they represent Jake's idealized vision of his relationship to Vickie. She is shown as his possession. In the movies, Jake is shown buying Vickie gifts, appears pleased with her as the bearer of his name and children, representing him as he wishes. In the objective representation of this change, Jake never is sure of his possession of Vickie.

The film's third visual style of representation, Jake's slow-motion perceptual subjective sequences, reveals his obsessive fears that his home movie fantasy of marriage to Vickie is flawed by the nightmarish feeling that he cannot completely control her sexuality. The disparities among these visual representations of their lives add up to Vickie's unknowable status as sexual commodity to Jake.

The first objective narrative sequence in which Jake worries about his ownership of Vickie occurs when she innocently remarks that a fighter with whom Jake is matched, Tony Janiro, is "good looking." This drives Jake into his first overt suspicions about Vickie's marital fidelity. Scorsese stages a conversation between Jake and Joey, in which Jake receives Joey's tacit agreement that "Any woman, given the right time and the right place, will do anything." Jake and Joey agree that, whenever Jake is in training, Joey will "watch" for "anything," a net sufficiently encompassing to make even innocence appear suspect. While Jake is training for the Janiro fight, Joey spots Vickie walking into the Copacabana with Salvy and a group of people. This sequence, one of the four in which Jake is not present but remains a felt presence, intensifies the ambiguity of the film's vision of Vickie. We, with Joey as Jake's representative, wonder why she would go out with "people that hate" Jake, as she puts it. Several technical elements of the film influence our consideration of her behavior at this point: the atypicality of the movie shifting away from one of Jake's multiplied points of view as well as the cause-effect sequential narrative logic of, first, Jake arguing that any woman will do "anything . . . at the right time" followed by the sight of her out secretly with Salvy – all of these elements combine to create doubt about her behavior.

While Scorsese multiplies Jake's perspective through the film's three cinematic styles – the objective narration, Jake's perceptual subjectivity sequences, and his fantasized depiction of his relationship with Vickie in the home movies – he divides, bifurcates, or refracts Vickie as an image while the film remains uninterested in her subjective experience of life with Jake. In six sequences, Scorsese photographs Vickie in images that construct a motif of dividedness and unknowability for her. First, when we and Jake first spot her at the swimming pool, she is separated from Jake by the group of Salvy and his friends; as Jake ogles Vickie that first day, Scorsese fetishizes her body. Shots linger on her face and hair and then upon her legs splashing in the water. Second, when Joey introduces Vickie to Jake, they are separated by the pool's chain link fence; they can actually only shake fingers instead of hands through the fence's links. Third, as Jake takes Vickie for their first ride, Scorsese shoots the scene as a tracking shot from in front of the car. At first, she separates herself from Jake by her polite, good girl distance from him on the front seat; she is also divided from Jake by the metal centerpiece of the convertible's front windshield that effectively separates the two within the frames. When Jake tells, not asks, Vickie to move closer to him, her image is then bifurcated by this same centerpiece, leaving Jake in full frame with her face divided in two. Fourth, on this first "date," Jake improbably brings Vickie to his parents' home, knowing the apartment is empty. Vickie initially sits at the opposite end of a very long kitchen table where she seems tongue-tied with shyness and Jake with sexual desire. As he always does, Jake directs Vickie's every move: He tells her to move closer. She moves to a chair on the front side of the table, now with her back to the camera. At his further urging, she sits on his lap. This unity, both in these literal frames of the film and more generally in their relationship, does not last long. Fifth, and the most dramatic of these images, is Joey's backing Vickie into a three-way mirror at the Copa when he sees her out with Salvy and friends. She is refracted into four different images: three in the mirror panes and one at whom we stare, wondering why she has chosen to go out with the very man her obsessively jealous husband despises. The sixth, final image occurs later in the film in Miami when Vickie tells Jake that she is leaving him. Vickie is inside the driver's side of her convertible with the top up. Her face is obscured both by the interior darkness of the car compared to the blazing sunlight of the Miami morning and by the windowpane of the car, which she has rolled up three quarters of the way to protect herself from Jake.

These six images of dividedness and unknowability visually parallel Jake's own cultural- and gender-biased inability to know his wife.

Jake's primitive conceptual categories for women do not let Vickie bridge the gap between sexual fetish, and wife and mother. This situation remains particularly true for Vickie with Jake because she maintains her highly sexualized appearance after she becomes a wife and mother. Given Jake's psychologically and culturally determined behaviors, it will just be a number of years and a number of battles before his jealousy, rage, and infidelity make Vickie leave him. Scorsese's film remains visually ambiguous about Vickie's fidelity while demonstrating, at the same time, that Jake is psychopathically jealous. Still, we continue on the journey with Jake, even as we watch him brutalize his loved ones.

Scorsese also employs both narrative structure and editing pace to increase the film's bond between Jake and us. In structure, the film demonstrates a rough parallelism between Jake's boxing career and his relationship to Vickie. In the early courtship and marriage years until her Janiro remark, Scorsese crosscuts among scenes with Vickie, home movies of Vickie and Jake, and Jake's fights presented as a string of victories moving toward the middleweight championship. Scorsese shoots these matches as a montage with a fast-paced upward trajectory toward the first middleweight championship fight that suggests the couple is happy together and that Jake has little trouble winning the matches. Act 2 functions as a tense, plateaued period in Jake's career in which he is now shown scrambling to meet weight limits for fights, as in the Janiro fight training. Here, Jake begins to struggle in both his relationship and his career. Increasingly, Jake's suspicions about Vickie with other men parallel his battles in the ring as Scorsese choreographs Jake's matches in longer, more brutal sequences that show Jake taking much more punishment in the ring. A sadomasochistic tone then governs both his domestic and boxing lives, with Jake dishing it out at home and taking it in the ring, as if he were paying for the first with the second and thereby maintaining our sympathy. This protracted tension throughout Act 2 comes to a climax in the hotel sequence prior to Jake's first title bout with Marcel Cerdan.

This bout has been scheduled as an outdoor match, and rain has delayed the fight's date. Scorsese shoots the hotel scene claustrophobically to make us feel that everyone in Jake's family and staff is stifled and nervous inside the hotel suite. The tension mounts as

Tommy comes by to wish Jake well before the fight. Scorsese shoots another slow-motion surveillance gaze by Jake of Vickie as she kisses Tommy goodbye. Objectively, nothing appears out of line in their kiss and Tommy's compliment of her trophy wife status ("Look at that face; just as beautiful as the day I met her"). But Jake's perceptual subjectivity dominates the scene. Innocent behavior photographed in slow-motion photography to represent Jake's intense perceptual lens of distrust reinforces doubts in the reader's mind that have been raised by previous slow-motion surveillance scenes of Vickie. This doubt is the consequence of the film's use of camera and narrative focus coupled with star power directed toward Jake as protagonist. The film shows us Jake objectively and subjectively as well as excluding objective interest and subjective point of view from Vickie. The narrative consequences of this slow-motion surveillance of Vickie – the steps the story takes next – are Jake's now familiar questioning of her public behavior as not sufficiently demonstrating his complete ownership of her. The conversation shifts to an argument between Jake and Joey about what Vickie will order from hotel room service, a scene that Scorsese shoots literally over her head. She sits on the couch while the brothers stand on either side of her arguing about her as if she were a piece of property. The hotel sequence slams to a conclusion when Jake's pre-fight jitters take sufficient offense at Vickie's display of herself as a sexual trophy and Joey's presumption to know better what to order for his wife. After a tense shouting match, Jake announces that he's "disgusted with the two a youse" and slams the bedroom door on both Vickie and Joey.

During this protracted stage of public and domestic tension, as Jake must wait for his first championship match and doubts his complete possession of Vickie, she becomes increasingly opaque in accounting for her behavior, then openly hostile toward Jake's emotional oppressiveness and physical abuse. This change is subtle. There is a greater patness in her responses to his inquisitions about her behavior while she is away from him; this is coupled with expressions of frustrated perverseness in giving voice to Jake's worst suspicions about her infidelity. The change results in less screen time for Moriarty than when she and Jake were in the courtship and "home movie" stage of their relationship. Further, because the objective narration never shows Vickie alone to reveal her as a subject of interest to the film, we know only how it looks to be abused by Jake. She remains a respondent to Jake, frightened and angry, but does not become a feeling subject of this abuse. Such exclusions create distance from Vickie; if we have any emotions about her, we wonder why she remains with Jake, but the ways in which she is represented in the film block us from empathizing with her.

The film's longest domestic battle, at Jake's Pelham Parkway home after winning his first championship title in 1950, takes place in four movements. It begins with an argument between Joey and Jake about Vickie; then it escalates into an argument and fight between Vickie and Jake. The fight climaxes in Jake's attack on Joey in Joey's home in front of Joey's wife and children, and it ends with Vickie reconciling with Jake. In this sequence, Scorsese relies on patterns he has already established for Jake. His angry look at Joey signals an impending altercation. We've learned, from as early as his first fight with Irma, that there will be repeated questions, rage, explosive physical abuse, and reconciliation. This entire "Pelham Parkway, 1950" sequence, from start to finish, lasts just over nine minutes; it feels like an eternity. What distinguishes this battle is its intensity; it feels much longer in its duration, as though Scorsese had protracted time. However, it is, with some editing when moving between Jake and Joey's houses, shot in real time. What also marks this battle as decisive is Joey's subsequent refusal to make up with Jake, quitting his job as Jake's manager, and exiting Jake's life.

The Pelham Parkway fight, in its entirety, represents what we infer are many more fights like this one. Jake appears for the first time after winning his middleweight belt as already overweight, with stomach protruding over Bermuda shorts, sandwich and beer in hand. The argument begins with Jake's accusatory confrontation of Joey for kissing Vickie on the lips when he greets her. This precipitates Jake's interrogation of Joey about the real cause of Joey's fight with Salvy at the Copa. Because this fight is one of the very few sequences that Scorsese shoots in which Jake is not present, we know more than Jake does about the fight. We are, then, encouraged to compare Joey's version of the argument with what we actually saw.

Jake initiates his investigation with a long, suspicious look at Joey, who is out of frame. Throughout this entire sequence, Scorsese uses only shot/reverse shot editing of the brothers. That they are never together in the same shot silently emphasizes their psychological distance despite their close physical proximity. Jake is obsessively examining past history in his ongoing effort to "just catch [Vickie] one time doing something [to betray him]." His question suggests that he regards Joey with this same suspicion: "Why didn't you ever tell me about what happened between you and Salvy at the Copa?" Joey proudly boasts about his assault on Salvy that night at the club. Significantly, he omits his reason for attacking Salvy – because he was with Vickie. Joey directly lies, saying that the fight had "nothing to do with Vickie." His dissemblance to Jake can certainly be explained as an appropriate response to an obsessively jealous, rage-aholic husband. However, our knowledge of its contradiction to what actually happened in the objective narration creates ambiguity and reinforces a reading of Vickie's behavior as possibly transgressive and certainly unknowable.

Jake's interrogation continues, fueled by information that may or may not be true. After Joey insists that the incident had nothing to do with Vickie, Jake counters with "That's not what I heard." He never discloses what he may or may not have really heard; he simply asserts that he "heard things," displaying an all-encompassing paranoia that viewers may doubt at the same time that we may also have doubts about Joey's reasons for lying to Jake. His own worst enemy, Jake compulsively drives on: "Did Salvy fuck Vickie?" to which Joey responds with an exasperated "Don't start your [obsessive Vickie jealousy] shit." Jake's paranoia, insinuation, and escalating threats crowd out our consideration of Joey's lie to his brother. Jake asserts that he doesn't "trust nobody" when it comes to Vickie; he then issues an all-encompassing threat: "If I hear something, I'm gonna kill somebody." Joey's response conveys anger and exhaustion: "Go ahead, kill somebody; kill Tommy, kill Salvy, kill me while you're at it." Unrelenting, Jake reads a psychological significance into Joey's syntax, which, without naming his causal logic as Freudian, demonstrates his belief that Joey has made an unconscious slip. He insists that Joey doesn't even know what he meant by including himself as the third direct object of Jake's threat to "kill" somebody. He infers that the sentence provides evidence that all three men "fucked" Vickie, asking Joey if he fucked his wife. Joey finds Jake's obsessive logic despicable, refuses to answer the question, and leaves, calling his brother a "sick bastard" for whom he "feels sorry." Although the scene feels much longer, it has taken six minutes.

Jake, left alone for a moment in his living room, then moves his interrogation upstairs to Vickie. Scorsese stages this fight with Vickie on her knees, at first because she is making up their bed. Her appearance is awash in images of light: her white blouse, platinum hair, and white bedclothes. With economical editing concision, Scorsese orchestrates this fight as shorter, louder, and more violent – building up to Jake's subsequent attack on Joey. De Niro repeatedly delivers his tense dialogue in soft-spoken language that instantly segues into violence. Jake begins by softly touching Vickie's hair, asking her what happened at the Copa. She, immediately on guard against Jake's rages, tells him she doesn't know what he is talking about. Jake lifts her to her feet by pulling her ponytail upward. Less patient than Joey, Vickie demonstrates to the audience that she has found her voice when grilled by Jake. In a two-minute sequence, she moves from guardedness to snarling insults. When he repeatedly slaps her face, she calls him a "fat pig selfish fool."

In moves that Moriarty conveys as often-repeated escape gestures, she quickly slips out of Jake's grip and locks herself in the bathroom. Vickie shouts for Jake to "Get away." When she refuses to unlock the door, Scorsese orchestrates a shot that demonstrates Jake's physical prowess and abusiveness in one moment. He smashes the bathroom door off its hinges to the floor in one gesture, sweeping into the bathroom toward Vickie, slapping her repeatedly. Vickie's frustration and rage are evident. While Jake repeatedly slaps her, she alternatively answers "Yes, no; what do you want me to say?" She taunts him by saying she "fucked them all – Tommy, Salvy, your brother, the whole street." Her taunts appear motivated by Jake's irrationality, cruelty, and violence. As he descends the stairs, she screams out one last insult, his brother's "cock is bigger than yours." Their battle continues outdoors as Jake marches to Joey's home while Vickie runs out into the street barefoot, trying to stop Jake. He pushes her down to the sidewalk, out of our sight because of a car Scorsese parks in front of the couple. This additional abuse is off screen, behind the car, but in the increasing shorthand with which Scorsese photographs their fights, it is just as distressing that we only hear Jake slapping Vickie.

Jake's physical attack upon Joey occurs in Joey's home in front of Joey's wife, children, and Vickie. This scene takes less than one minute and is so compellingly vivid that it feels much longer. Scorsese shoots much of Jake's attack from the floor, from Joey's point of view. We don't actually see all the blows Jake lands upon Joey. Instead, we see Jake's deliberate, calm face as well as his fists and feet swinging and kicking at us as if we were Joey.

Scorsese deftly paces the overall Pelham Parkway fight sequence. An ominous, momentary lull occurs after Jake's horrific attack on his brother. An undetermined number of hours have passed as the scene opens with Vickie returning to their house to pack a suitcase. While Vickie enters and moves up the staircase in the back right of the frame, Jake is foregrounded in the front left screen, staring at a blank television screen in the unlit gloom of the living room, a truly disturbing sight. When Jake follows Vickie into the bedroom to beg her to stay, Scorsese stages Jake's successful reconciliation in less than two minutes. As opposed to his dominance in all three previous segments of the battle, Jake here shares the frame with Vickie, behind her, touching her gently at her waist, nearly whispering his pleas for her to remain. What astonishes us, and must therefore sway us back to Jake, is Vickie's quick, unspoken acceptance of Jake's entreaties. What sways her must, to some degree, also sway us, and De Niro's presence is very powerful. Drawing upon the tight coherence of the film's psychological portrait of Jake, this sequence structurally echoes Jake's pattern of inquisition, explosion into self-righteous violence, and seconds later, a turnaround to peaceable husband who wants to get along, played out with Irma, his first wife, over the cooked steak.

Scorsese ends this brutalizing domestic abuse sequence with a sound overlap and smash cut to the last round of Jake's 1950 fight with Dauthuile, wherein Jake has been taking a vicious beating only to turn around in the last round and knock Dauthuile out to retain his title. This is the first time Scorsese represents Jake really having to get hurt to win his matches. Paralleling the downward spiral of his marriage to Vickie, Jake's fights in the second half of Act 2 are both much harder for him to win and much harder for us to watch. Because the Dauthuile beating follows the protracted domestic fight scene, cause-effect narrative logic suggests that this professional beating is connected in some way to the domestic abuse we have just seen him administer. His pain in the ring becomes an unconscious punishment for what he does at home; it is a sign of his losing battle to retain ownership of Vickie, given his abusive, jealous nature.

Quickly following the Dauthuile struggle is the film's final bout between Jake and Sugar Ray Robinson in which Jake loses his championship to Robinson. Bringing to a climax Jake's boxing career in the film, this fight is at once the most violent and most highly stylized of all of Jake's matches. Intensifying the downward turn of Jake's boxing career initiated by the damage he must take to win the Dauthuile match, Jake doesn't just lose to Robinson. Scorsese crucifies Jake in this match – with attendant religious solemnity and symbolism. To maintain the rhetorical hold De Niro exerts as La Motta, even as he is losing his middleweight championship, Scorsese photographs the fight with a variety of techniques that demand our attention. Slow-motion photography emphasizes the force of the blows Robinson lands repeatedly on Jake's body, capturing Jake's facial distortions as he absorbs each blow. The infamous blood- and saliva-spewing of the matches is at its peak here. At one point, a punch explodes Jake's face with such force that the camera follows a long, heavy splatter of blood dousing the audience. Vickie is so appalled by Jake's beating that she is forced twice to cover her face with her hands and bend her head to her lap. Scorsese shoots the most compelling perceptual subjectivity shot in the entire film in the final moments of this match. We watch Robinson from Jake's point of view as he waits for Robinson to strike a deadly blow to Jake's face. Perversely, Jake eggs Robinson on: "Come on, Come on, Come on, Ray." Scorsese thus turns La Motta's loss of the title into a quintessential Scorsese film moment: the eagerness with which violence is dispensed and even anticipated. Emphasizing the religious solemnity and symbolism, Jake's trainer swabs his blood-soaked sponge in blood, no longer water, and squeezes the bloody water-shot in slow motion down Jake's back. Finally, the match is called. Jake, however, has the final word: no longer human-looking from his facial disfigurement, Jake staggers over to Robinson to insist that, even in defeat, he "never went down."

The match sequence ends with the famous shots of the empty ring, with the blood-soaked rope dripping in slow motion. Although the film showed some of Jake's matches ending in losing decisions, this is the single fight in which Jake is resoundingly beaten. In defeat, La Motta has never appeared more heroic. These two brutal matches, back to back after the terrible domestic fight sequence, suggest an unspoken but powerful narrative logic. Jake is subconsciously driven to take abuse in the ring as compensation for the abuse he dispenses at home. Thus, while he is spiraling downward in both his domestic and professional lives, he is somehow rhetorically redemptive of the audience's sympathy, even after terrorizing his family, by his steely ability to withstand the pain.

THE NIGHTCLUB WOMEN

The film shifts to Act Three, Jake's nightclub years in Miami, as abruptly as the lighting and mise-en-scene change from the dark, bloody Robinson match to the blinding white sunlight flooding Jake's Miami backyard swimming pool. Act 3's women stand radically apart from Vickie throughout Act 2. Whereas Vickie, as enacted, creates psychological havoc for Jake because he can never know with certainty that she is his sexual commodity, the club women of both the Miami and New York parts of Act 3 are unknown – not unknowable as she is, just unknown because they are of no interest to Jake as possessions. They are use objects only, rentable in sexual and economic exchange terms. In contrast to Vickie, he has no interest in owning their sexuality, just exchanging it for some laughs, some booze, and some money. They have no names, no separate identities, and are closer to Irma, Jake's first wife, in that they are uninteresting to him. Thus, he expends no energy surveilling and investigating them. For Jake, Irma was known but of no interest; Vickie was unknowable and thus, he was never sure that he ever completely possessed her. The club girls are the complete opposite of Vickie, but a step lower than Irma: they are unknown and uninteresting. The role of women essentially ends with Vickie's departure, as do Jake's rages. In Act 3, the club women aren't worth his psychological investment, and among other narrative ends that are loosely tied up, Jake appears to be generally calmer, although not especially happy. The screenplay suggests that Jake's eclarissement occurs in the Dade County Jailhouse after his arrest for letting two fourteen-year-old girls drink in his bar. His final raging bull scene shows him pounding his fists into the concrete wall because he is so angry with himself for his carelessness. His recognition must be inferred from the quiet, then sobbingly repeated, declarations he makes to himself after his rage: "I'm not an animal; I'm not an animal; I'm not an animal." Scorsese's complex but undeniably heroic rhetoric dominates this scene; the director does not linger on Jake's low point or the interior meaning of Jake's declaration to himself. The scene ends with a dialogue overlap from the subsequent scene in which Jake is already back in his club, telling a joke to the audience.

Although it is obvious that Jake, not women, is the central focus of *Raging Bull*, it is not evident except through analysis of technique exactly how Scorsese creates and maintains Jake's power over the narrative. The multiplication of his perspectives, coupled with the film's exclusion of voice or subject status to Irma, Vickie, or the club girls in the objective narrative, ensures that we know what Scorsese wants us to know about Jake's career and his private life. Because the film gives none of these women any status but that of reactor to Jake in the objective narration and no perceptual subjectivity sequences, we remain trained on Jake's feelings and more removed – because we are technically distanced – from the women's feelings. From watching the film, we know that living with Jake La Motta was a traumatic experience, but we do not learn this directly from the woman's perspective. As a naturalist work, *Raging Bull* shows Jake as both a product of his personality and his environment. However, Scorsese's cinematic technique also enables De Niro as Jake to break free of those determinist factors through Scorsese's magnificent rhetorical techniques designed to win our admiration for Jake's courage and savage power. The women remain the most controlled characters in Scorsese's naturalist, neo-Neorealist world because he never allows them to break free, as does De Niro's Jake, to establish themselves as feeling subjects of the film. Boxing is a tough game, and the techniques Scorsese uses in *Raging Bull* to depict one boxer's professional and domestic world shows how tough it can be on the women in his life.

NOTES

1.   Laura Mulvey, "Visual Pleasure and Narrative Cinema," in *Visual and Other Pleasures* (Bloomington: Indiana University Press, 1990), 14–26.

2. Wayne C. Booth, *The Rhetoric of Fiction* (Chicago: University of Chicago Press, 1961), 274, 188, 279–81.

3. Aristotle, "Poetics," in *Critical Theory Since Plato*, ed. Hazard Adams (New York: Harcourt Brace Jovanovich, 1971), 31.

4. See, for example, Noël Carroll, *The Philosophy of Horror or Paradoxes of the Heart* (London: Routledge, 1990), 158–59, on horror's magnetic attractiveness for us.

5. Jake La Motta, Joseph Carter, and Peter Savage, *Raging Bull* (1970; reprinted, New York: Bantam, 1980), 7, 5.

5 My Victims, My Melancholia

Raging Bull and Vincente Minnelli's The Bad and the Beautiful

Despite the many transtextual moments in *Raging Bull*, its engagement with Vincente Minnelli's *The Bad and the Beautiful* (1952) has largely escaped critical attention. When Scorsese put together his meditation on American cinema, *A Personal Journey with Martin Scorsese Through American Movies* (1995), he chose to begin the four-hour documentary with a clip from Minnelli's film about a megalomaniac Hollywood producer and three victims of his boundless ego. Many years before this, in *New York, New York* (1977), Scorsese shot a violent car scene in homage to one of the emotional high-points of *The Bad and the Beautiful*.[1] In *Raging Bull* itself, allusions to Lana Turner in *The Postman Always Rings Twice* (1946), Kirk Douglas in *The Champion* (1949), and Minnelli as director of *The Father of the Bride* (1950) inevitably lead us to consider *The Bad and the Beautiful* – the tale of angst-ridden Hollywood masculinity in which the three stars combine forces. Furthermore, in those key moments of desire in *Raging Bull*, when Vickie dangles her legs in the pool and later over the foot of the bed, Scorsese makes reference to the first thing we see of Lana Turner in *The Bad and the Beautiful* when her legs (also her entrée in *The Postman Always Rings Twice*) hang down from a hole in the roof of an abandoned Hollywood mansion. Given the obvious importance of the film both to Scorsese and to the iconography of *Raging Bull*, critical neglect of *The Bad and the Beautiful* in this context offers a surprising and challenging oversight.

The real importance of the comparison of *The Bad and the Beautiful* with *Raging Bull* lies in what it tells us about the melancholic hero of popular film and the characters that become his sacrificial victims. Such a comparison also emphasizes the extent to which films about the male melancholic, such as *Raging Bull* and *The Bad and the Beautiful*, draw on mythical narratives of melancholia as analyzed by Freud in *Mourning and Melancholia* and *Totem and Taboo*. This chapter will address these issues. Very little has been written on the melancholic hero, yet he is central to the films of Martin Scorsese and particularly *Raging Bull*. As Fred Amile (Barry Sullivan), Georgia Lorrison (Lana Turner), and James Lee Bartlow (Dick Powell) are used by Jonathan Shields (Kirk Douglas) to feed his creative fantasies in *The Bad and the Beautiful*, Vickie and Joey are compelled by Jake to indulge strange fantasies of his own. Both films give a qualified validation of their reprehensible male protagonist, despite the damage he inflicts upon those who love him. Where *The Bad and the Beautiful* differs and is instructive, however, is in the fact that it focuses greater attention on Fred, Georgia, and James Lee and the effect of, what Thomas Elsaesser calls, their "manic manipulation" by Jonathan.[2] Narrated by each of them in turn, unlike Vickie and Joey, they have a clear voice in the film to tell their own stories and to demonstrate how those stories are central to Jonathan's. *Raging Bull* and its critical reception are largely concerned with Jake and his point of view. A reading of the film that takes *The Bad and the Beautiful* into consideration, therefore, reminds us that there is another story unfolding in Scorsese's film. This is the story of Joey and Vickie as Jake's victims. Comparison of the two films encourages us to read their story, and it also helps us to understand the extent to which Jake and Vickie's story of oppression is vital to Jake's narrative. This is to acknowledge that any attempt by the spectator to validate Jake's experience and regard him as a redeemed figure, as Scorsese does, can only be made at great cost.[3] This is because at the center of Jake's story lies the pain and suffering endured by Vickie and Joey as the puppets in Jake's performance of loss. However much we may validate the suffering of Jake and his own status as victim, it is Joey and Vickie who are the real victims of Jake's mean and melancholy history.

Elsewhere I have argued at length that, subdued by an overwhelming sense of loss, the Scorsesean male protagonist is invariably melancholic.[4] The central defining features of Scorsesean melancholia are, first, that the melancholic experiences a sense of separateness from a corrupt and conservative group, such as the Italian-American Mob (*Casino* [1995]), nineteenth-century New York society (*The Age of Innocence* [1993]), or the twentieth-century New York crowd (*Taxi Driver* [1976]); second, he undergoes the trauma of loss, frequently represented by the loss of a desired woman (*Bringing Out the Dead* [1999]), but also loss of a desired male (*Mean Streets* [1973]) or even the loss of a country (*Kundun* [1998]); third, he refuses to relinquish mourning of that loss and erects a mental crypt, a private space where he can preserve his love for the lost object of desire (*Life Lessons* [1989]) or where he can play out a narcissistic fantasy scenario of his own popular importance, power, and authority (*King of Comedy* [1982]) – both allowing the Scorsesean melancholic a place where he can indulge in fetishization of that loss[5]; fourth, he displays an ultimate desire for conformity with the group effected through an overt show of self-sacrifice or renunciation (*The Last Temptation of Christ* [1988]); and finally, he benefits from the consolidation of personal authority and power through the workings of melancholia and the public recognition of his private fantasy and self-inflicted stoicism (*New York, New York*).

Raging Bull is the Scorsesean melancholic text *par excellence.* The key opposition between the melancholic and a conservative, almost tribal, group is clear in Jake's struggle for independence from the Italian-American Mob, represented in the film by Tommy's decaying family. In his stubborn refusal to accept either the Mob's help or its conditions in gaining a title fight, Jake nominates a realm of personal, moral, and perhaps even spiritual values that, he believes, set him apart from the lazy corruption of the Mob. Obviously a man of incredible physical prowess, Jake's sense of separateness from the Mob is further emphasized when we consider the aging and diminutive characters of Tommy's family who are attempting to bring Jake into line. Their eventual success in gaining his conformity – making him take the "dive" (such as it is)[6] – provides Jake with a minor note of loss, an inevitability from the beginning of the film for the contender who would be champ. But this sense of loss is enfolded, in Jake's melancholic fantasy, with the more substantial loss of Vickie and Joey and the Darwinian horde-family they complete under his rule as animal patriarch. This is a fantasy family much like that of Charlie (Harvey Keitel) in *Mean Streets*, which includes the an-archic Johnny Boy (Robert De Niro) and Charlie's cousin Teresa (Amy Robinson). Here, in relation to *Raging Bull*, Freud's account of the origins of civilization in *Totem and Taboo* is useful for an understanding of Jake's fantasy, his horde posturing, and his struggle with the Mob, which bears a strong resemblance to Freud's post-horde band of brothers.[7]

Jake's horde posturing – clearly indicated in the Copacabana face-off between his horde and Tommy's group – forms the basis of his fantasy scenario (Figure 18). Having lost his horde family, a loss confirmed by his personally meaningful, but objectively pointless, act of self-sacrifice in his final fight with Sugar Ray Robinson, his melancholic crypt-work of loss-fetishization alters. His private (because publicly incomprehensible) refusal to let go of the horde family, which represented his power, gives way to a public performance of loss in his night club act. We see part of this act – the recitation of the *On the Waterfront* (1954) speech – in private, but the stage hand (played by Scorsese) tells Jake that the Barbizon Plaza, where he is performing, is crowded. By the end of the film, Jake's melancholia has clearly gained public recognition and his blameworthy life has achieved a validation that, as Pam Cook points out, easily sees our desires fused into Jake's own.[8]

In many ways, Jonathan Shields in *The Bad and the Beautiful* fits the melancholic description. Setting up a personal war with the Hollywood establishment that hated his father, Jonathan demonstrates his personal vision and opposition to the Hollywood mob in his stated ambition to "ram the name of Shields down their throats." This sense of a personal vision is a fundamental feature of male desire in Minnelli's films and a number of his heroes counteract their obvious sense of loss with an attempt to build their own world. For Elsaesser, this is Minnelli's "great theme": "the artist's struggle to appropriate external reality as the elements of his own world, in a bid for absolute creative freedom."[9] Loss pervades Jonathan's narrative both in the death of his father and in the more obscure form of the "after picture blues," which he explains to Fred early in the film.[10] Just as he hires Hollywood extras as mourners at his father's funeral, in "Shields Productions" Jonathan creates an elaborate fantasy entity,

17. "You've got to give the Devil his due."

which includes Fred, Georgia, and James Lee, as a public and ongoing memorial to the loss he experiences in the very act of film production. In pursuit of this expensive and exploitative melancholic fantasy, Jonathan loses everything: Fred, Georgia, and James Lee, in particular. This is where the film begins and ends. At this point of loss, however, Harry Pebbel (Walter Pidgeon) articulates Jonathan's gesture of conformity with the Hollywood establishment. To revive his career and his fantasy scenario of loss, he must crawl to Fred, Georgia, and James Lee, who are now very much a part of that establishment. If they agree to work with him once more, despite the past, Harry can raise the money to get Jonathan's show back on the road. All three refuse, seemingly hammering a highly effective nail into Jonathan's coffin of loss. As they leave Harry's office, however, Jonathan is still on the phone from Paris, excitedly narrating his latest story idea to an impatient Harry. Overhearing this, his greatest enemies are strangely moved to pick up the extension to hear his ideas. Once again, they are captivated by Jonathan's pitch and, at this point, we know that they will work together again (Figure 17).

18. "I got a problem.... "

Despite everything, the melancholic victimizer achieves a seemingly impossible redemption. This validation will lead to another
Shields production and yet more opportunity for public recognition
of Jonathan's private story of loss.

The initial Hollywood outsider status of Fred, Georgia, and James
Lee in *The Bad and the Beautiful* provides something of the desired
difference and separateness central to Jonathan's fantasy. When Fred
and Jonathan first meet, Fred is a tongue-tied, aspiring filmmaker,
barely scratching out a career on Poverty Row and yearning for the
opportunity to become a great director. In Georgia's case, as she says,
when she met Jonathan, she was neither a woman nor an actress –
she was a drunk, financing her habit by picking up bit parts from
people who knew her father, a Barrymore-styled former movie great.
By contrast, James Lee was a successful college professor and best-
selling author, deeply suspicious of Jonathan and Hollywood and
highly resistant to being suborned by either. Lending Jonathan their
frustrated ambition, personal suffering, and non-conformity, these
characters augment Jonathan's quest for a mythic persona of radical
individualism. As Hollywood outsiders, Fred, Georgia, and James Lee
help in the production of Jonathan as the creative "genius boy" of
new ideas and new, young people – a sensitive and understanding
man apart from the rigid conservativism of the Hollywood in-crowd,
a man who does things in his own way.

The key significance of Joey and Vickie in marking Jake's difference, and his separation from Tommy and Salvy's all-male group, lies in Joey and Vickie's taboo status. In the terms of *Totem and Taboo*, this is the extent to which the Mob has decreed that they cannot be touched (*SE* 13: 25). When Jake first sees Vickie at the pool, Joey describes the effect of her taboo. Vickie may well "hang out" with Salvy and his crew at the pool, but as a fifteen-year-old girl of precocious physical beauty, she does not "go with them." At the Chester Palace dance, we see her and a single female friend, lone women among Salvy's larger crew of men. We see such a configuration again in Tommy's group at the Copacabana, although this time without Vickie. There, a lonely female figure sits silently with her back to the camera. In both cases, the minority female presence works to regulate desire in the all-male group. When she is part of Salvy's gang, Vickie stands for desire in the group, and she provides the group with a powerful point of sublimation of that desire.[11] But, although desired by all, she cannot be possessed by any single individual of the group without risking jealousies and the outbreak of socially disruptive violence (*SE* 13: 144). She must therefore be shared by all, and in a non-sexual way. The bearer of such a powerful taboo, she may not be touched. The bearer of such a taboo – a menstruating woman, for example – is feared in totem societies as unclean or dangerous, a compromised second-class citizen. The fact that Jake incorporates her within his possessions is sign enough of his desire for difference (*SE* 13: 23). But his violation of the group's unspoken taboo over her is a potent sign of his separateness from the group. As no single member of the group would dare claim her as his own, by doing just this, Jake powerfully asserts that he is not a member of such a group. Vickie's continual presence among Jake's possessions simply emphasizes the fact.

A great deal has been written about homoeroticism in *Raging Bull* and particularly about the conflation between fighting and sexual exchange in the film.[12] Jake brings the various strands of this discussion together when, fed up with the continual assertion of Janiro's good looks, Jake quips, "I've got a problem. I don't know whether to fuck him or fight him." Of particular interest in the homoerotic discourse surrounding *Raging Bull* is Jake's love and sexual desire for Joey. The essence of this relationship is potently expressed early in the film when, having banished his first wife from the room, Jake forces Joey to punch him repeatedly in the face. When Joey finally stops, having re-opened the cuts to Jake's face sustained in a previous bout, Jake pinches Joey on the cheek. The significance of homoerotic exchange in the film, for our purposes, is to further indicate the use he makes of Joey to mark his status as taboo violator. A general homosexual/homosocial identification may well exist in a band of brothers like Tommy's Mob family (*SE* 13: 144), but beyond the kind of sublimation we have commented upon in relation to Vickie, homosexual exchange in such situations can only ever be threatening to the stability of the all-male group. When Salvy sees Jake and Joey fighting in the training ring, he remarks, "They look like a couple of fags." It is, therefore, this double taboo of incest and homosexuality that Joey's presence in Jake's horde suggests. As the general violator of such taboos, Jake's status outside the conservative Mob-group and its laws, as well as his pretense towards the power of the pre-taboo horde patriarch, is again confirmed by his possession of Joey.

In Jonathan and Jake, we see that melancholic loss is no singular event in their narratives. For the melancholic, loss does not begin or end a narrative: it pervades. Despite the three points of loss in *The Bad and the Beautiful*, the temporal pervasiveness of melancholic loss is indicated in the film by way of the initial flash-back to Jonathan's public mourning over his father. In *Raging Bull*, there is a strong contrast between the fit and muscular Jake of the opening credit sequence and the fat and flabby Jake of the mournful night club years. This similarly begins the film with the idea of loss being as evident in Jake's youth as it is in his maturity. Despite everything that happens in the plots of the two films, both films give clear indication that there was never a time when their protagonists were not subject to the pains of loss.

In its cyclical nature, *The Bad and the Beautiful* emphasizes the melancholic's need to continually restage his habitual sense of loss by proxy. That continual need, which Scorsese demonstrates with each new melancholic text, Minnelli demonstrates in one film. It is in this proxy role that Fred, Georgia, and James Lee show themselves to be very useful indeed. Each character is jettisoned from or repelled by Jonathan, and all display their moments of suffering as a result. Fred stands in the background, stunned by betrayal, as Jonathan walks away with his directorial replacement, Von Ellstein (Ivan Triesault). Georgia speeds off recklessly and almost mortally in her car after she finds Jonathan with Lola. James Lee brutally slugs Jonathan after he hears of his former friend's role in the death of his wife. Thus, each character is given an experience of loss by Jonathan as part of the process of offsetting and augmenting his own. In attempting to master the loss of his father and the loss he feels in the after-picture blues (when directors, stars, and writers obviously become redundant to him), Jonathan nurtures loss and suffering in his loved ones, which he then reclaims as part of his own expanded sense of loss. His reaction at their moments of departure – especially in his painful speech of self-justification to Georgia – suggests this, and the fact that the film begins with his yearning for their return makes it clear. Thus, taken up by Jonathan's own sense of loss, they become recipients of some of that loss only to have it reclaimed by Jonathan as his own. In this complex example of what Nicholas Abraham and Maria Torok have called melancholic introjection, the melancholic Jonathan takes on and stages, as his own, their grief at having lost him.[13]

In *Raging Bull*, Jake's overriding sense of loss is obscure, but in addition to the deprecation of taking the dive for Tommy, loss is similarly centered on Vickie and especially Joey. As in *The Bad and the Beautiful*, however, this is a loss for Jake that he himself has brought about. His desperate and psychotic need to assume the status of a cuckold (another state of masculine impairment) brings him to deal out a violent and savage physical punishment to Joey and Vickie, which ends his relationship with his brother and brings on the beginning of the end with his wife. Nevertheless, despite his obvious culpability in the matter, in his fantasy scenario, Jake casts himself as an almost passive victim of deprivation. The self-sacrifice he stages in the following Sugar Ray Robinson fight is a complex emotional event for Jake and lends itself to a variety of interpretations. In this context, however, it is highly instructive of the process whereby Jake marks the loss he has inflicted on others as his own loss. That is to say, long playing the role of the victimizer, his fantasy can easily turn the situation around to cast himself as the victim – exactly the opposite of his usual boxing strategy of initially playing "'possum," weathering a continual stream of blows but at the same time wearing down his opponent, before finally inflicting a stinging attack and gaining a knock-out victory. Allowing himself to be beaten by Sugar Ray, as he beat Joey and Vickie previously, he is both admitting his guilt and, more importantly, incorporating the suffering of his victims to bolster the public recognition of his own suffering. In this way, acting as both man and animal, Jake casts himself as the self-sacrificing god of regeneration.[14] His extreme and masochistic gesture is thus cast, at least in his own mind, as the redemption of all humankind. The effect is augmented by his less violent, but emotionally extreme, night club routine, where he glibly wears his heart on his sleeve, parading his loss for both money and applause. In both performances, Jake invokes Joey, Vickie, and the extreme victimization he has visited upon them as talisman-like objects of loss to give a clearer form and meaning to his more abstract feelings of loss.

Perhaps the best metaphor for the callously self-serving nature of Jake's relationship with Joey and Vickie is to be found in the familiar Hollywood film figure of the greedy and covetous producer – of which Jonathan in *The Bad and the Beautiful* is a perfect example. James Naremore has detailed the associations made between Jonathan and Hollywood figures, such as Orson Welles, David O. Selznick, and indeed the infamous Broadway producer, Jed Harris.[15] In the mythscape of personal obsession surrounding all three figures, we can observe a useful model for Jonathan's obsessive drive to lure Fred, Georgia, and James Lee into his productions, to bleed them dry, and then let them go. The incredible measures he takes to procure them (especially Georgia and James Lee) are only superseded by the methods he employs to obtain what he wants from them. He deceives Fred to get *The Far Away Mountain* into production; he panders to Georgia's love for him to secure her best possible performance; and he puts his in-house Latin love in the way of Rosemary Bartlow (Gloria Graham) to free-up James Lee and get their script written. For Jonathan, no moral or ethical impediment is too great to impede getting what he needs for the fantastical ego projections that are his films.

The extreme and unscrupulous methods Jonathan employs to secure Fred, Georgia, and James Lee for his production family tell us a great deal about their worth to him. As we see with the mink-lined Milo (Nina Foch) in Minnelli's *An American in Paris* (1951), Jonathan seems to need his victim-protégés in an obsessive and highly possessive way.[16] The insanity of this need is demonstrated by the fact that, initially, only James Lee has anything like a track record of achievement to warrant such a need. Beyond this, their real worth to Jonathan is hardly demonstrated in their work, which, in each case, is entirely reliant upon Jonathan's significant input. What he gets from them, of course, are cheap and vulnerable projections of his own ego – the puppets he needs to stage his fantasy scenario. Their apparent lack of natural talent merely indicates the callousness of Jonathan's victimization.

Just as Jonathan needs Fred, Georgia, and James Lee to play out roles in his films, Jake requires Joey and Vickie to make up the numbers in his horde fantasy. Like Jesus' in *The Last Temptation of Christ*, Jake's horde-family is defined by the presence of woman and children, as opposed to the all-male Mob trying to claim his allegiance.[17] As head "gorilla" of the horde, the very thing Salvy calls Jake at the Copacabana, Jake's fantasy places his as the supreme authority and not subject to the Mob's Oedipal regime based on the consensus of equals (*SE* 13: 141–144). Vickie's role in this horde is undemanding but vital. The extent to which Jake relies on her presence, not so much as a taboo possession won from the Mob but as the mother of his horde, is clear in two scenes following outbreaks of violence. In the first of these scenes, Jake fights with Vickie over the good-looking Janiro and banishes her from the kitchen where he is discussing the upcoming fight with Joey. On Joey's advice, however, Jake goes to make up with Vickie, now on the floor in the sitting room with the children. There he moves around on his hands and knees, kissing Vickie and the babies, as Joey's wife Lenore sits at the side with her own brood. The short scene strongly resembles the horde group of a dominant gorilla (*SE* 13: 141). The second of these scenes follows the violent beating (mentioned earlier) that Jake gives Joey and Vickie. Some time after, Vickie returns to the house and makes ready to leave him. Penitent, Jake implores her to stay, saying, "I'm a bum without you and the kids." Despite all his actions to the contrary, the fact of Vickie's lowly status as possession is thus demonstrated to be vital to Jake's self-image and the terms of his struggle. The presence and sole possession of women and children in his horde is vital to his fantasy of separation from the Mob group, which thoroughly regulates and virtually forbids the enjoyment of such pleasures (*SE* 13: 143).

Joey's role in Jake's horde fantasy is more complex. He remains central to the horde ideal so long as he remains a feminized and infantilized figure,[18] that is, so long as he follows Jake's orders and allows himself to be Jake's possession. He is driven out, however, when he is suspected of infringing upon Jake's rights as ape-like head of the horde, that is, when Jake suspects him of infidelity with Vickie (*SE* 13: 141). In both the breach and the observance, however, Joey serves the horde idea of Jake's bizarre delusions. Even in his business negotiations with Salvy and Tommy – which Jake's paranoia sees only as an act of betrayal – Joey serves Jake's fantasy of a horde versus Mob struggle. Like the gangster genre itself, Jake's own fantasy narrative of horde loyalty and order is best served not when the group is working smoothly, but when it is on the point of decay, a situation consistent with Freud's observations about totemic order (*SE* 13: 9). In so far as Jake's paranoia sees Joey as betraying him to Salvy and Tommy, Joey plays a vital part in affirming the truth of such a struggle in Jake's mind.

The idea that Joey and Vickie are objects of loss for Jake relies on his ability to re-cast their deprivation as his own deprivation, rather than his fault. The same situation applies to Jonathan in relation to Fred, Georgia, and James Lee in *The Bad and the Beautiful*. But the idea that the male melancholic has caused the departure of his victims, that he has forsaken them, is also useful to his performance of loss. That is, in so far as Joey and Vickie represent, in Jake's bizarre fantasy scenario, the facts of his non-conformity (his maintenance of a horde operating against Tommy's Mob), eradicating them indicates his self-sacrifice designed to mark his ultimate reconciliation with the establishment. The same goes, in relative terms, for Jonathan and his gang. In *The Bad and the Beautiful*, Harry makes constant reference to the good that has come from Jonathan's bad. Elsaesser reinforces this view, to a certain degree, reading Jonathan as "destroying their private lives" to liberate their previously imprisoned creative potential.[19] Listening to Harry, it is as if the megalomania behind Jonathan's betrayal of Fred, Georgia, and James Lee has had little effect beyond the beneficence it has bestowed on the Hollywood community. It is as if these acts of betrayal are only Jonathan's various moments of self-sacrifice which, in the successful careers of Fred, Georgia, and James Lee and in the two or three films of Jonathan's that take their place in the Hollywood top ten, have indicated his commitment not to self but to the great Hollywood motion picture industry.

For Jake, in the terms of his bizarre and obscure fantasy, the eradication of Joey and Vickie leaves them not just figures of his loss but also markers of his self-sacrifice. They are sacrificed to his need to *make* a sacrifice. Given that Jake once saw them as so vital to his horde and hence key to his resistance to Tommy's Mob rule, their removal marks the end to his resistance and his god-like gift of self-sacrifice on behalf of the wider community (*SE* 13: 153). The actual effect of this sacrifice in the world around Jake is, of course, negligible. Beyond initially requiring him to take a dive, the Mob has no real interest in Jake. As we see in the absence of Tommy and Salvy at the all-important final Sugar Ray fight, Tommy and his family have no real sense of the sacrificial terms in which Jake has cast his fantasy. Nor are they present to witness it.[20] As Freud observes, such a fantasy scenario for the melancholic is carried out under no other direction that the melancholic's own narcissism (*SE* 14: 250).

I have already discussed the response registered by Fred, Georgia, and James Lee to Jonathan's outrages against them. These are brief but, particularly in the case of Georgia's automania, powerful indications of their suffering. After their time with Jonathan, much of the rest of the film for Fred, Georgia, and James Lee is really marked by a sarcastic and smug attitude towards him. Beyond a brief shot of Georgia wearing a mourning costume at the beginning, there is no indication that any of them have spent much of the intervening years lamenting the past. As Minnelli brings their stories to the fore, however, Scorsese augments the portrayal of the suffering of Jake's victims to greater levels.

Given Georgia's automaniacal departure from Jonathan's life in *The Bad and the Beautiful*, it is indicative of the inter-penetration of these two films that Jake's last moments with Joey and Vickie are also staged around cars. Just as gossip columnists rumored that Lana Turner's fourth marriage ended in a fight in a parking lot,[21]

Vickie announces her departure from Jake in his Miami night club car park. Certainly it is a bitter departure but, as an indicator of her discontent, it is nothing like the bitterness of the final encounter with Joey to come. This is not to dismiss Vickie, finally, as a legitimate victim of Jake's fantasy. The bruises and the blows she has sustained throughout the film speak for themselves. What it does reflect is the way Jake uses his victims and spits them out when they no longer serve the cause of his melancholia. It also reflects the misogyny that underpins Jake's narcissism, which in turn reveals the ideology of the homosocial Mob group to which he will give his ultimate allegiance. In this way, Jake conflates his objects of loss into the single loss of his brother, Joey. Joey is, after all, a more suitable object of memorialization for the melancholic who, like Jonathan Shields and his father complex, ultimately seeks to renegotiate his contract with patriarchy rather than terminate it in favor of an alternative identification.

Jake's last encounter with Joey is in a New York parking lot. This encounter shows Joey's discontent and indicates his criticism of the melancholic fantasy for which he has been used. When Jake first sees Joey, after so many years, Joey gives him the cold shoulder. Jake follows him, however, and compels him to turn around, forcing himself and his embrace on an obviously unwilling brother. Following this awkward exchange, Joey reluctantly agrees to call Jake in a few days, but it is obvious that he does not mean it. His enduring bitterness at his former victimization is made clear when Jake tries to kiss and be kissed by Joey and Joey says to him, "Let me call my wife and kids. Don't you want them to see the kiss?" Whether it is Jake kissing Joey or the reverse, Joey understands how his brother's fantasy operates. The kiss Jake expects demonstrates his desire to perform publicly and be celebrated as the sensitive and complex man of sorrows. Joey's wife and kids saw Jake's violent and humiliating attack on Joey. Now Joey mockingly suggests they should bear witness to Jake's performance of remorse. Joey's resistance to his brother's bombastic affection is understandable. Having been so badly abused, why should Joey allow Jake the opportunity of demonstrating openly his capacity for sorrow, pain, and atonement, which, from Joey's perspective, are probably insincere emotions? For Joey to reciprocate Jake's affections, in front of his own family, would only serve to validate further the melancholic's desire to wear his grief publicly. This is, of course, the very thing Jake does in his night club performances. Here we see not only a potent display of Jake's melancholia, but also the central importance of Joey (who, by this stage, is also a surrogate for Vickie) to this performance.

Jake's night club performances represent a pathetic display of personal loss. In no other context could Jake more dramatically parade his melancholia than in these bars and clubs – low-life dives – where he performs his rise and fall as a boxer. What little we see of his routine is dry, repetitive, clichéd, and cribbed; it continually rehearses and restages his career as a boxer, intermingling this sad tale with melancholic allusions to a liberal selection of authors, including Shakespeare, Tennessee Williams, and Rod Serling, the author of *Requiem for a Heavyweight* (1962). Jake's place in the world outside his private fantasy is unstable and, as we see in the Florida stockade scene, easily slips into madness. Lacking in expression and sophistication, his night club routine is not far removed from the animal cries and wall-beating of the stockade scene. Twice we see Jake perform before an audience, both times rehashing old chestnuts about wives cheating on their husbands – another potent allusion to his own cuckolding by Joey and Vickie. In the final scene, which is also the opening scene, we gain a more substantial insight into Jake's complete story and the central importance of Joey and Vickie's stories within it.

In the solitude of the dressing room, Jake's fantasy is emphasized, in part, as a solitary one. Unlike Jonathan, whose performance of loss is almost always a public expression, Jake's performance may even exist for no one but himself. The stockade scene emphasizes the extent to which Jake is fighting with himself. The drab isolation of the dressing room conveys a sense of hopelessness but shows that Jake is somehow satisfied in his fantasy world – "I'm the boss" he repeats as easily as he asserted the fact before he became champ. Jake's loneliness, matched with his optimism, imbues the scene with a sense of pathos. His struggle against the Mob, to assert what he considers to be his right to a horde and supreme authority, has been thoroughly defeated, and yet Jake still believes in the truth of his own vision. To the spectator, Jake is a figure of pity, perhaps even a sympathetic figure believing in him when all those around him have forsaken him. To this extent, the lone melancholic, seemingly repentant figure attracts our indulgence.

In neither the stockade scene nor the dressing room scene is the spectator privy to Jake's private state of mind. His actions in both scenes merely replicate and rehearse the performances he has made all his life, before huge audiences. The Barbizon Plaza may not be Radio City Hall but, despite some of the seedy bars Jake has performed in, the Barbizon suggests that, in the 1960s, people were still coming to hear his melancholy history. When Scorsese, as the stagehand, tells Jake that the house is crowded, we know that we are not the only ones who have come to hear and see Jake's performance. Jake's isolation, his struggle to maintain his inner vision, is opened out by a wider public willingness to hear his story. Like Jonathan's films in *The Bad and the Beautiful*, Jake's fantasy scenario, the creation of his own world, thus gains a wider cultural legitimacy and validation, despite the cost to its victims, Joey and Vickie.

By placing his own story in amongst those of other boxers and "great men" of film and literature, Jake sees his tale as part of a wider cultural tradition – perhaps even of mythic significance. In this way, Jake's night club performances play a significant part in his melancholic display. Like the stories he draws upon, Jake's performance represents a continuation of his struggle against what he perceives as injustice. It also continues his fight for pre-eminence with the Mob and to possess a horde of his own. But as we know, this struggle has been long since lost. What the night club performances achieve is the mastering and validation of that loss. There is also a clear element of theater to Jake's shows. Just as Jake continually played possum in his boxing career, as he allowed himself to be sacrificed in the ring, Jake's night club routine restages his loss for the pleasure and applause of others.

Jake's final recitation of Brando's speech from *On The Waterfront*, with its heavy emphasis on the blaming of the brother, indicates his failure to deal with the reality of his own violence towards Joey (and Vickie). Furthermore, it demonstrates the way Jake uses Joey, above all, as an alibi for the memorialization of his own personal loss.[22] The performance ignores any aspect of the suffering Joey has endured and conjures a fantasy picture of him as a sign of the loss of Jake's horde and a focus for his nostalgia and hostility. For Jake, the loss of Joey represents the loss of the horde and the defeat of his desire to be something better than Salvy, Tommy, and the rest of the decrepit Mob.

Joey's hostility at seeing his brother marks the victim's outrage at his former role as object of the melancholic's history. Jake's narrative, his achievement and demonstration of melancholia, is maintained at the expense of Joey and Vickie. Jake's wider narrative thus incorporates the melodrama of punishment and victimization endured by his wife and brother. Joey's hostile response to his brother is largely explained by the punishment he received at Jake's hands; it is also this drama that has created the context in which Jake's melancholia has been achieved and displayed. Thus, it is Joey's response as Jake's victim, the loss that he and Vickie represented well before they abandoned Jake, which largely drives the melancholic narrative. Just as Jonathan's loss-by-eradication of Fred, Georgia, and James Lee enabled the development of Shields Pictures, the loss of Joey, which begins and ends the film, provides the essential matter of the melancholic narrative; here, Joey's implied castigation of Jake evokes that sadistic victimization Jake once dealt out to Joey and Vickie, which continually renews and gives strength to Jake's melancholic fantasy.

In *The Bad and the Beautiful*, we never see Jonathan's intended production. His request for Fred, Georgia, and James Lee and their interest in the project suggest that it might look something like Jake's routine – another installment of the male melancholic's story of loss, financed on the exploitation, brutalization, and sacrificial eradication of his favorite victims. Where it will differ from Jake's performance piece is that Jonathan needs his victims in person. His detached presence, by telephone, at the end of the film, like Freud's murdered and subliminated god father of the fraternal band (*SE* 13: 143), suggests an awareness that his own memorialization of loss (the next film) will be staged largely by the living faithful Fred, Georgia, and James Lee. The fact that Scorsese does not use Minnelli's secondary source approach to tell Jake's story is indicative of the fact that the Scorsesean melancholic really only needs his victims as an idea. This fact indicates their ultimate exploitation. Whereas Jonathan requires warm bodies on his set to achieve his fantasy, Jake's narcissism populates its own world. Requiring not even the presence of Joey and Vickie, Jake's melancholic fantasy exists most powerfully as nothing more than an eternal thought in the mind of the melancholic Scorsesean hero.

NOTES

I am most grateful to Ali Wirtz and Barbara Creed for their invaluable comments and suggestions.

1. James Naremore, *The Films of Vincente Minnelli* (New York: Cambridge University Press, 1993), 134.
2. Thomas Elsaesser, "Vincente Minnelli," *Genre: The Musical*, ed. Rick Altman (London: Routledge, 1981), 19.
3. Some conflict has emerged between Paul Schrader, one of the writers of *Raging Bull*, and Scorsese as to the question of Jake's redemption or salvation. Scorsese indicated his position with the concluding quotation from John 9:24: "All I know is this: once I was blind and now I can see." Schrader commented, "I don't think it's true of La Motta either in real life or the movie." See Les Keyser, *Martin Scorsese* (New York: Twayne, 1992), 121.
4. Mark Nicholls, "Martin Scorsese's *Kundun*: A Melancholic Momentum," *Metro*, no. 116 (1998), 11–14; Mark Nicholls, "Something For the Man Who Has Everything: Melancholia and the Films of Martin Scorsese," *Playing the Man: New Approaches to Masculinity*, ed. Dave Trudinger, Katherine Biber, and Tom Sear (Annandale, Australia: Pluto Press, 1999), 39–51, 215–216; and Mark Nicholls, *Scorsese's Men: Melancholia and the Mob* (Annandale, Australia: Pluto Press, 2004).
5. Lesley Stern, *The Scorsese Connection* (London: BFI, 1995), 224.
6. Carol Siri Johnson, "Constructing Machismo in *Mean Streets* and *Raging Bull*," *Perspectives on Raging Bull*, ed. Steven Kellman (New York: G. K. Hall, 1994), 101.
7. Sigmund Freud, *The Standard Edition of the Complete Psychological Works of Sigmund Freud*, ed. and trans. James Strachey, 24 vols. (London: Hogarth Press, 1955–1974), 13: 140–146). Hereinafter cited parenthetically as *SE*.
8. Pam Cook, "Masculinity in Crisis," *Screen*, 23 (1982): 3–4.
9. Elsaesser, "Vincente Minnelli," 15.
10. Naremore, *Films of Vincente Minnelli*, 127, sees this as manic depression.
11. David Friedkin, "Blind Rage and 'Brotherly Love': The Male Psyche at War with Itself in *Raging Bull*," *Perspectives on Raging Bull*, ed. Steven Kellman (New York: G. K. Hall, 1994), 122–130.
12. Compare Robin Wood, "The Homosexual Subtext: *Raging Bull*," *Australian Journal of Screen Theory*, 15/16, pp. 57–66, and Friedkin, "Blind Rage," 122–130.

13. Nicholas Abraham and Maria Torok, "Mourning or Melancholia: Introjection versus Incorporation," *The Shell and the Kernal: Renewals of Psychoanalysis*, ed. Nicholas T. Rand (Chicago: University of Chicago Press, 1994), 136.

14. In Freud's reading of the Mithras slaying, in *Totem and Taboo*, the god commits the deed in the sacrifice of the father, acting alone to redeem the company of brothers from complicity in the original deed (*SE* 13: 153). This, of course, is precisely the nature of Christ's sacrifice of the cross.

15. Naremore, *Films of Vincente Minnelli*, 112.

16. Elsaesser, "Vincente Minnelli," 19.

17. Lorraine Mortimer, "Blood Brothers: Scorsese, Schrader and the Cult of Masculinity," *Cinema Papers*, no. 75 (September 1989), 35.

18. Johnson, "Constructing Machismo," 102.

19. Elsaesser, "Vincente Minnelli," 25.

20. Compare Richard Librach, "*Mean Streets* and *Raging Bull*," *Film / Literature Quarterly* 20 (1992): 14–24.

21. Sam Kashner and Jennifer Macnair, *The Bad and the Beautiful: Hollywood in the Fifties* (London: Little, Brown, 2002), 255.

22. Pam Cook, "The Age of Innocence," *Sight and Sound*, February 1994, 45–46, uses the word "alibi" to describe Ellen Olenska in *The Age of Innocence*.

Reviews of *Raging Bull*

"RAGING BULL: NO PUNCHES PULLED"

Jay Scott

The Globe and Mail [Toronto], 15 November 1980, Entertainment section, p. 3, reprinted with permission from *The Globe and Mail*.

As Jake La Motta, a world champion welterweight prizefighter whose career collapsed in the mid-fifties, Robert De Niro brings to Martin Scorsese's new film *Raging Bull* (at the Uptown) one of the most astonishing metamorphoses in the history of movies: he ages by more than 20 years and balloons by more than 40 pounds – *real* pounds – in the space of two harrowing hours.

When we first see La Motta under the credits (*Raging Bull* is in glorious black and white, save for a few home-movie sequences in faded color), he is warming up in the ring in 1941 and De Niro is clearly in the best shape he has been in his life. A title (New York City, 1964) appears and Scorsese cuts to a dressing room in an unidentified theatre where a paunchy, gross-featured figure with a battered puss that has the texture of potato skin is reciting doggerel in front of a mirror: "So give a stage/Where this bull here can rage." As the camera glides toward the face, recognition comes slowly: poked into the almost monstrous flab are two porcine eyes that could belong to Brando, or James Caan. De Niro flashes his goofy, moronic grin and one accepts the incredible.

The story of Jake La Motta, rags to riches to rags, is an actor's dream, but both De Niro and Scorsese have been careful not to make their palooka into a conventional (or even an unconventional) hero. Violent, vindictive, volatile, childish, and psychotically jealous of his beautiful second

135

wife, a succulent blonde named Vickie (Cathy Moriarty), La Motta is portrayed in a melodramatic format – an *homage* to Warner Brothers of the thirties – that deliberately suggests tabloid newspapers and newsreels.

Scorsese achieves his remarkable effects through surprisingly modest means. Period music ("Big Noise" from Winnetka, Monroe singing "Bye Bye Baby") is used sparingly; the original score is MGM pastoral (the lyric theme recalls "Over the Rainbow" in both melody and orchestration). There are simple but stunning visual contrasts between De Niro's *café au lait* skin tones and the creamy vanilla of Miss Moriarty's cheeks. La Motta's slippery grasp of reality is signalled by photographing scenes of Vickie through La Motta's eyes, in slow motion – very fast slow motion, a nearly imperceptible shift of speed. Where *Rocky* and *Rocky II* saw boxing as a groaning waltz of dinosaurs (Rocky Balboa was a heavyweight), the battles in *Raging Bull* are jitterbugs of death danced by stinging insects – quick, vicious, blistering exchanges of venom.

Overall, *Raging Bull* is so tough (it is, however, restrained in comparison to Scorsese's most expressionist exercises, *Taxi Driver* and *Mean Streets*) and so intransigently anti-romantic that some viewers are certain to wonder why it was made at all. Where's the *moral*? Twice married, La Motta beats both wives and throttles Joey (Joe Pesci), his long-suffering brother, when he paranoically decides Joey has been fornicating with Vickie. La Motta is not a nice guy; *Raging Bull* is not, and does not want to be, a nice movie – Scorsese is after verisimilitude, not myth.

(Sexual possessiveness and its inevitable vitriol, the strong subtext of *Raging Bull*, has always been a major motif in Scorsese's work. The most illuminating example is perhaps *Taxi Driver*, where Scorsese himself plays one of Robert De Niro's fares. He orders De Niro to park outside a highrise, points to two figures silhouetted in a window and calmly informs De Niro the figures belong to his wife and her black lover. He is going to kill both of them, he says. Jake's attitude toward Vickie in *Raging Bull* is neither as concentrated nor *quite* as pathological; in all other respects, it is identical, and it, more than the boxing, gives *Raging Bull* its edge.)

Miraculously, La Motta's relationship with his wife survives the beatings – for the time being – though the relationship with his brother does not. Retirement provides a nightclub in Miami (called Jake La Motta's, of course) and it seems likely the old pro will settle into a reasonably profitable and pleasantly easy dotage. Except that the old pro, who has turned his free-floating hostility toward his patrons and does a stand-up comedy routine – he's an unfunny Don Rickles precursor – is allergic to the profitable, the pleasant, the easy and the reasonable. The boxer who gratuitously smeared an opponent's nose "from one side of his face to another" because Vickie found the opponent "good looking" is not about to stay out of trouble.

In the scene that climaxes De Niro's performance, La Motta has been thrown into the Dade County Jail. For the first time, the fighter sees the brick wall – the prison of his own personality – he has been shadow-boxing all his life, and he bangs his head and his hands into the concrete blocks lining his cell over and over again, screaming, "Why?! Why?!" The intensity of the film verges on the intolerable.

Hemingway would hate *Raging Bull* – it's about the life of boxing, not the art – and many of the men in yesterday's audience who had come for a true-life *Rocky* and who had originally egged La Motta on regardless of his activities (a tantrumy up-ending of the dinner table set by the first wife was greeted with cheers and applause) were finally bludgeoned into silence by Scorsese when their hero had become aged and corpulent and unmistakably cruel. La Motta lost them, but De Niro didn't; one may lose empathy for the bruiser, but one never loses sympathy for the human being. "I wanted this film to be real," Scorsese has said, and in his smoky primal world, heroes are something taking up space on TV sets in the background. When La Motta, in the neatest, sickest joke of the movie, appears at a benefit and reads the "I coulda been a contender" speech from *On the Waterfront, Raging Bull* comes full circle: Jake La Motta was champion of the world, but he's one of the world's champion losers. And he's still raging.

"RAGING BULL"

Eric Gerber

Houston Post, 19 December 1980, p. 1E, reprinted with permission.

For a boxing movie that devotes less than 15 minutes to in-the-ring action footage, *Raging Bull* still leaves you feeling as though you had ducked and winced through a full two hours of on-screen punches. It's a tribute to this unblinkingly brutal biography of fighter Jake La Motta that what happens outside the ring is usually as powerful and exciting as the brief, but brilliantly staged boxing excerpts.

Director Martin Scorsese (working from La Motta's autobiography via a screenplay by Mardik Martin and Paul Schrader) has, you should excuse the expression, pulled no punches in *Raging Bull* and fashioned what is probably the most grimly accurate exercise in biography Hollywood has yet allowed the public to see. Compare this boxing biopic of the 1948 middleweight champion to, say, *Somebody Up There Likes Me* (Paul Newman as Rocky Graziano) which is a good film, but one that has re-fashioned Graziano's life (and boxing itself) to accommodate the rise-fall-rise romanticism that conventional Hollywood filmmaking demands.

There is absolutely nothing romantic about *Raging Bull*, beginning most immediately with Scorsese's decision to film in black and white. (Poor United Artists! First, Woody Allen decides to go b&w on them and now Scorsese. Next thing you know, Sylvester Stallone will announce he's not using color for *Rocky III* and Cubby Broccoli will decide James Bond might do better in b&w, too). But it's too simple a description to label *Raging Bull* as realistic (or Realistic, for that matter). As with what he did most notably with *Taxi Driver* before this, Scorsese accents certain elements of his stringent material and approach in an expressionistic manner. All that means, practically speaking, is that he occasionally uses off-speed camera work (slowing down an action to emphasize the deep impression it is making on the character's consciousness), utilizes music in an ironic context, and – most obviously – stages the fight sequences as compressed bursts of violence that effectively capture the physicality of the entire bout.

If there is a literary genre that *Raging Bull* resembles, it is not Realism, but 19th-century Naturalism with its unyielding pessimism and man-as-animal motif. At the beginning of the film, when La Motta (as played by Robert De Niro) is still a young fighter, he jokes with his brother-manager (Joe Pesci) about being "an animal." Toward the end of the film, when a grossly overweight and long-retired La Motta is thrown in jail (on a morals charge) we see him beating his head against a wall and moaning, "I am not an animal." In between, we see enough to make us inclined to agree with his original assessment.

La Motta is depicted as a man whose primary virtue as a boxer was his ability to withstand an inordinate amount of punishment. His opponents would often grow arm-weary and exhausted battering him around. The one time the head-strong La Motta goes along with the mob and throws a fight (in exchange for a title shot), he simply stands there, arms down, and lets Billy Fox take shot after shot. And when he loses his middleweight crown to Sugar Ray Robinson, – by a late-round TKO – a bloody, savaged La Motta staggers over to the victor and punch-drunkenly boasts, "I never went down! Ya never got me down, Ray!"

His other chief personality trait was a vicious temper that channeled itself most often into near-psychotic feelings of jealousy regarding his young wife (whom he married at 15). An idle remark from her that one of his opponents was "good looking" prompts him to intentionally disfigure the young fighter. Eventually, he accuses his ever-loyal brother of adultery with her and beats him up and that's the end of their relationship.

As has been much publicized, De Niro underwent some strict physical conditioning to play the boxer La Motta in his prime (it paid off; De Niro is a most convincing fighter), then turned around and gained some 50 pounds or so to re-create him in the later years when he's retired from the ring and become a kind of celebrity buffoon, opening a night club and doing a stand-up comedy routine. Has there ever been another actor who went to such lengths in preparing for a role? More importantly, how necessary is it really? I can't argue with the results – seeing the overweight De Niro is startling in just the way Scorsese wants it to be – but such preparation raises bothersome questions, to say the least.

De Niro is more or less guaranteed another Oscar nomination from this performance (deservedly so), but equally deserving is Joe Pesci for his quiet portrayal of La Motta's put-upon brother. This is a classic example of an unknown actor exploding in a role that seems to have been tailor-made for him and vice versa.

Thus far, this has been a disappointing Christmas season as far as films go, but *Raging Bull* stands as the one unqualified success so far. It is, to be sure, not the kind of upbeat holiday entertainment many desire right now, but it is disturbingly excellent and easily one of the year's best films.

FROM "MUSCLEMEN"

Michael H. Seitz

The Progressive 45 (February 1981): 50–51, reprinted by permission from *The Progressive*, 409 E. Main St., Madison, Wisconsin 53703. <www.progressive. org>.

Martin Scorsese's *Raging Bull* is possibly the best American movie of the past year. It is a work of great intensity, boasting superlative acting in the major roles, a number of memorable and finely staged scenes, rare (if misplaced) artistic conviction – and it continues to haunt me some weeks after my first viewing.

The title refers to the 1970 autobiography of Jake (the Bronx Bull) La Motta, one-time middleweight boxing champion. The film, however, is less an adaptation of La Motta's book (written with Joseph Carter and Peter Savage) than a representation of Scorsese's and star Robert De Niro's view of him. Yet despite a few historical inaccuracies and transpositions, it does follow the major lines of the boxer's career.

La Motta grew up as a poor Italian boy in the Bronx, landed in reform school, and began a professional boxing career in the early 1940s. He was a rough, brawling, and not especially artistic fighter, who both took and gave a great deal of punishment in the ring. In 1947, according to La Motta's own admission, he threw a fight to Billy Fox (for which he was briefly suspended by the Boxing Commission). But this dive, ordered by the Mob, earned La Motta a shot at the middleweight title. This he won in 1949, then lost in 1951 to the great Sugar Ray Robinson.

After the Robinson fight La Motta's life both in and out of the ring went into a swift decline. He abandoned training, put on weight, and in 1954 had to retire from boxing altogether. In the meantime he had managed to alienate just about everyone around him, and had moved to Florida with his children and second wife, Vickie (a cool blonde sex-pot, whom he married when she was only fifteen). Vickie took the kids and left him, however, after he opened a sleazy bar in Miami Beach and began indulging in heavy drinking and extra-marital affairs.

This blow was followed by arrest on a morals charge – allowing a fourteen-year-old girl to operate as a prostitute out of his bar – for which La Motta was sentenced to six months in the Dade County stockade. Apparently, the humiliation of this experience had a profound effect on him: By 1964, La Motta had returned to New York, performing in a night club act.

Although *Raging Bull* traces the major events of La Motta's career, it is not really a fight movie. Only about fifteen minutes of the film's two-hour running time depict action in the ring. The movie shows almost nothing of the rigors of training, and does not represent enough of any single fight for the viewer to get a sense of it as a strategic or dramatic contest. What prizefighting we do see comes as stylized renderings of pugilistic violence, enhanced by selective use of the camera and electronic manipulation of sound.

Most significantly, Scorsese maintains a neutral attitude toward the violence unleashed in the ring, and does not use these scenes for emotional arousal. The viewer is not encouraged to feel either revulsion or excitement over the ring's bloody spectacle, but is merely asked to accept it as a representation of the brutal, animalistic world in which La Motta lives.

The principal emphasis of the film is on the fighter's life outside the ring, especially as seen in his relationships with Vickie (Cathy Moriarty) and his brother Joey (Joe Pesci), who worked in Jake's corner and acted as his adviser. *Raging Bull* is thus essentially a film biography, but it differs from most works in the genre by its refusal to glorify the life it portrays. Nor does the film seek to explain La Motta's dark and often self-destructive urges through facile psychobabble.

The Jake La Motta whom Robert De Niro so palpably brings to life is an unattractive, unthinking, inarticulate brute. Yet he is also a human being, made of all too mortal flesh – something La Motta himself doesn't seem to realize until the time of his wretched incarceration. "Why?" he wails alone in his cell – and by the very act of posing this question manifests, however minimally, his tortured humanity. And as he repeatedly pounds his head and fists against the wall, he cries out in agony, "I'm not an animal!"

Scorsese has found in La Motta's life an example of the possibility of redemption, even in the most unlikely cases. The film, he has said, is a tale "of a guy attaining something, and losing everything, and then redeeming himself."

If this view of La Motta reflects Scorsese the one-time seminarian and would-be priest, still haunted by a Catholic notion of sin and redemption, *Raging Bull*'s cinematic realization also reflects the artistic sensibility of Scorsese the obsessed film and image junkie. ("He breakfasts off images," director Michael Powell has observed, "and eats tapes for lunch.")

The film, much of which was made on New York locations, has been shot in wonderfully gritty black and white. This gives it a look distinctive among other contemporary films, yet reminiscent of the period with which Scorsese is dealing. Our memories of the 1940s and early 1950s, after all, are inextricably fused with those of black-and-white movies and early television. The black-and-white narrative is intercut with several other sorts of images, equally associated with the process of recollection: clips from Jake's and Vickie's eight-millimeter color home movies, photographic fight stills, fight images on a television monitor. These varied *aide-memoires* serve to evoke what I take to be the film's thematic sub-text: the mysterious dynamics of memory and regret.

Raging Bull is both compelling and disturbing. I'm not sure I like it, nor am I entirely convinced that Scorsese and De Niro have invested their efforts in a worthy or fruitful subject. But I do feel that *Raging Bull* is one of few American films released in 1980 which merit serious critical discussion.

"DE NIRO PACKS A MEAN PUNCH: STUNNING BUT UNSENTIMENTAL, *RAGING BULL* SCORES A KO"

Philip Wuntch

The Dallas Morning News, 19 December 1980, p. 1C, reprinted with permission of *The Dallas Morning News*.

Martin Scorsese's masterful *Raging Bull* knocks you out and leaves you cold.

That, admittedly, is a rather sweeping statement to make about any film, but it sums up both the awesome grandeur and the slight weakness of *Raging Bull*. It does indeed knock you out, with both its technical brilliance and the strength of its boxing scenes.

But it also leaves you cold, in the traditional moviegoing sense of wanting a protagonist with whom identification is comfortable and even cozy. Robert De Niro's magnificent Jake La Motta is emphatically not Sylvester Stallone's Rocky Balboa. Although *Raging Bull* qualifies as a humane film, with its unspoken and unsentimental compassion for a largely trashed life, Scorsese avoids making a so-called human drama, along the lines of *Kramer vs. Kramer, Ordinary People*, or Scorsese's own *Alice Doesn't Live Here Anymore*.

Scorsese and De Niro insist viewers accept one-time middleweight champion La Motta without easy explanations or cliched apologies. He is presented as a man who must hurt someone – even, or perhaps especially, himself – to prove the mere fact of his existence. The reasons for his behavior are suggested by the endless noise of tiny apartments filled with votive candles and crucifixes, by the reeking atmosphere of New York street life, by the examples of pop culture emanating from the radio and by the chronic threat of Mafia infiltration. But they're never trivialized into armchair psychology.

As La Motta, De Niro gives his finest performance yet, overflowing with mean, brutal anger compounded by the frightened alienation of a gladiator who doesn't know who he may have to kill in the ring. The sound of his mirthless, hostile laughter is chilling. And in the film's pivotal scene, he sobs in his jail cell, almost quoting John Hurt's *Elephant Man*, "I'm not an animal." But it's the whimper of a truly lost soul rather than a ploy for compassion.

So much has been made of De Niro's 50-pound weight gain for the film's later scenes, and the publicity threatens to overshadow the merits of his performance. Suffice it to say that the device seems a natural extension of De Niro's character as an actor rather than a gimmick.

In the only other two roles of any footage, Cathy Moriarty and Joe Pesci excel as Jake's resilient second wife and his browbeaten brother.

Miss Moriarty, an untrained actress, has the natural spontaneity of someone not entirely conscious of the camera, and her occasional stiffness
only emphasizes the taunting haziness of her somnolent beauty. Pesci
convincingly plays the younger brother who will take only so much in
the name of fraternity and profit.

Scorsese, the most nervous of directors, has found a screenplay to
which his peculiar frenzy is suited perfectly. *Raging Bull* contains the
finest use of slow motion since *Bonnie and Clyde*, and the black-and-
white photography is appropriate for the gray world inhabited by the
film. The fight scenes, photographed from remarkably versatile angles,
are savage, primitive ballets, but the impact of their stylized violence is
staggering. Arteries really seem to burst, and blood spurts across the ring
and, it would seem, almost into the audience. The unorthodox use of
sound, going beyond the bone-crunching fury of most fight scenes, also
adds a new texture to the film.

The screenplay takes a newsreel approach to La Motta's life and hard
knocks, examining him at crucial moments and leaving the details to
viewers' imaginations. Considering the nature of the man, that may be
as close to Jake La Motta as one would care to get.

Raging Bull, one of the most stunning films of the year, opens Friday
at the UA Cine, UA Skillman Six, Promenade and Northtown Six.

"*RAGING BULL*"

Joe Pollack

St. Louis Post-Dispatch, 20 February 1981, p. 5D, reprinted with permission of
the *St. Louis Post-Dispatch*, © 1981.

There's a raw power to *Raging Bull* that sucks one in, as if into a mael-
strom where a nightmare begins, a nightmare filled with pain and violence, blood and tears.

It is a film that brings mixed feelings of fascination and revulsion – like
watching a trapped animal, hating its struggle and feeling its torment,
but unable to release it and unable to stop watching.

And it certainly is an effective film, Martin Scorsese's story of the life of
boxer Jake La Motta. In addition to eight Academy Award nominations,
its strength is shown in that much remains with the viewer, but so do a
number of questions.

The basic one is "Why?"

Why make the film? Why tell the story of this mean, ugly, vituperative,
vicious, unfeeling human being? Why lionize a man who, when he can't
find anyone else to beat up on, chooses his wife? Why make a hero of a

man whose life consisted of smashing his fists into other people's faces, but who could be eminently practical, ignoring the desire to win when it was more important to take a dive, to deliberately lose?

The answer belongs to Scorsese alone, but he has shared some of his thinking with us in his other films, primarily *Mean Streets* and *Taxi Driver*. He seems to be drawn by something in the the seamy side of cities and people, the not-quite-civilized part, the area where violence erupts suddenly, spontaneously, with less warning than Mount St. Helens and with almost as much devastation.

Scorsese seems enraptured by this world, taking an almost surreal pleasure in peering through the camera lenses, looking gleefully from his position of safety to the arena in which people are destroying one another, and themselves in the process.

And yet, *Raging Bull* is fascinating, made so by Scorsese's direction, the acting of Robert De Niro and Joe Pesci and by the special effects and slow-motion work of the fights themselves. The ring action is the most violent and authentic ever, if that is a praiseworthy statement. Blood flies from smashed noses, sweat from gloves and steaming bodies.

The action sequences are more realistic than in any other boxing film, including *Rocky*, although no one ever has brought the feel of sadness and deep, emotional pain to the ring the way John Huston did in *Fat City*.

There's another major difficulty to *Raging Bull*, and that involves the treatment of women. By La Motta's definition, backed by Scorsese and writers Paul Schrader and Mardik Martin, there are only two types of women – virgins and sluts, and as soon as one is no longer the former she immediately becomes the latter.

La Motta was married five times, but the film shows only two wives, Cathy Moriarty and her predecessor. De Niro pursues the blonde, 15-year-old beauty, wins her and divorces his wife to marry her. Then, of course, things change, and it is as if La Motta sublimates growing doubts of his masculinity in favor of loud and profane doubts of her fidelity.

Watching him punch her around is hardly a moment of charm.

As a fighter, La Motta was good, but not great. He was a brawler, willing to take two punches to give one, but as a boxer, he was not in Sugar Ray Robinson's class. Few were, of course, but La Motta probably was more than a notch below Robinson.

In addition to Oscar nominations for the film itself and for Scorsese as director, De Niro and Pesci are tapped for Best Actor and Best Supporting Actor, respectively, and if justice is to be served, Pesci should be a unanimous victor.

His portrayal of La Motta's brother, and at the same time his agent, his manager, his procurer, his protector – and sometimes his sparring partner – is simply marvelous. He is the only character in the film to show any depth, any humanity, and through a considerable amount of pain, he shows these characteristics beautifully.

Moriarty is pretty enough, in a Bronx blonde manner, but when it comes time to grow a little, to mature, she falls short.

De Niro, always a powerful actor, offers all the ugliness and violence that the real La Motta apparently exuded like a body odor, and it permeates everything. It looks as if he and Jack Lemmon (*Tribute*) will be one-two in the Oscar race.

Scorsese's use of black and white film makes the ring scenes more grotesque, if that is possible, with the only use of color a device, but an effective one. Grainy color footage, supposed to be home movies and looking like them, is used to show a passage of time and a growth of La Motta and family.

Most of the time, Scorsese emphasizes the bleakest sides of La Motta's character, and De Niro plays them to perfection.

Besides the blood and violence inside the ring, the rating undoubtedly stems from the almost-constant use of the crudest of gutter language outside it.

"*RAGING BULL* IS A GRITTY, BRUTAL MASTERPIECE"

Vern Stefanic

Tulsa World, 20 February 1981, p. C7, reprinted with permission.

Raging Bull is a superlative film, at least in technical terms, and it is probably the best movie about boxing ever made.

It is also brutal, both in content and in the graphic depiction of boxing violence, and some may be offended by its nature and frightened by its unflinching view.

Emotionally, *Raging Bull* might be too brutal for its own good. The hero (Robert De Niro, as prize fighter Jake La Motta) is almost totally unsympathetic. This man not only physically hurt his ring opponents, he also beat his brother and wife, and all these episodes are filmed in graphic terms.

It's not a pretty picture, and neither is this a "pretty" film. Viewers should be prepared: *Raging Bull* is a story of survival, both in the boxing ring and in the slums of the South Bronx, and the hero survives because he's mean.

It's also a movie with very harsh language. Very.

But in any case, it's a film to be remembered. It has been nominated for eight Academy Awards, including best picture, and the skill and dedication displayed on this work is staggering.

Raging Bull is based on the story of former middleweight boxing champ La Motta, a violent man with a passionate temper and bullish fighting style. He would absorb a flurry of punches from his opponents, just to land one himself.

The amount of punishment visible on screen during the fight scenes may have people reeling as they watch. Director Martin Scorsese gets his camera right into the ring, catching every facial expression and every devastating blow.

De Niro, one of this century's most dedicated and talented actors, gives a powerful performance, both in and out of the ring. His recreation of La Motta's bouts are incredible (he did his own boxing) and his character is complex and grimly realistic.

De Niro's La Motta is a tragic victim who gets even. Born into poverty, he fights his way to higher levels of society. He's also a man who, despite his boxing discipline, cannot resist temptations that ruin his life once the boxing career ends.

De Niro actually looks the part of a raging bull when the film begins; we first see him prancing in the ring, hypnotically captured with slow-motion photography, a picture of terrific energy waiting to be unleashed.

Then come the determined, bullish charges. The punches that devastate. The killer instinct that destroys.

And when De Niro's sitting at home with his wife, the same mood prevails. When he questions his brother about cheating with his wife, the killer instinct surfaces. It's a relentless performance.

There are two other outstanding performances here. Newcomer Cathy Moriarty makes her debut as La Motta's beautiful wife, and she adds dimension to what might have been a cardboard role.

Joe Pesci adds just the right restraint in his role as La Motta's younger brother and manager. Both he and Miss Moriarty have received Oscar nominations for their work.

But the real star, perhaps even more important than De Niro, is Scorsese, one of Hollywood's bona fide "whiz kids" who has specialized in films that painted a dark picture of everyday life.

Scorsese himself is a native of New York City's Little Italy, so he understands these people and their world. He didn't make a movie about foreign matters. The setting is his home.

Scorsese's familiarity with the Roman Catholic church is also evident, and it's no accident that one scene at a church neighborhood dance (where De Niro first longs for the beautiful Moriarty) is so authentic – right down to the young men's smiling but flagrant disrespect for a priest.

Scorsese uses several dazzling techniques to tell the story effectively. Most obvious is that the movie was filmed in black and white, because Scorsese wanted to capture the view of American boxing that was filmed on grainy newsreels.

Color is used twice. The title, *Raging Bull*, is in red (against the black and white background), and the La Motta home movies, used for exposition, are shown in color.

Scorsese also films several scenes in slow motion, effectively emphasizing La Motta's desires, be it a need to knock a man out or to win a girl's heart.

And during the boxing scenes we hear the sound of grunting, aggressive animals, an inspired move that reduces the boxing matches to a war of animal survival. There is no art in the ring, only sluggers who punch to avoid being punched.

The fight scenes are brutal and often painful to watch. Black blood flies from the cuts, and sound effects make each punch sound as if it had been delivered with sledgehammer force.

But the scenes are always realistic. There are no phony fight heroics in this work. It's an often horrible but always authentic picture.

Scorsese is a talented director (*Mean Streets, Taxi Driver, Alice Doesn't Live Here Anymore, New York, New York*) and this time he tops himself. He takes bold steps to make his film a powerful, visual masterpiece, and the gambles pay off.

Viewers might not like the story or the character portrayed by De Niro. *Raging Bull* is as much a story of how the American dream of success can turn sour as it is about boxing, and that's something people are not always anxious to see.

But there's no denying its technical brilliance and power. *Raging Bull*, after all, apparently wasn't made to entertain.

It apparently was made as a salute to – and example of – excellence in film making.

Filmography

WHAT'S A NICE GIRL LIKE YOU DOING IN A PLACE LIKE THIS? (1963)
Direction: Martin Scorsese
Screenplay: Martin Scorsese
Music: Richard H. Coll
Cast: Zeph Michaels, Mimi Stark, Sarah Braverman
Format/Duration: B/W, 16 mm / 9 minutes

IT'S NOT JUST YOU, MURRAY (1964)
Direction: Martin Scorsese
Screenplay: Martin Scorsese and Mardik Martin
Cinematography: Richard H. Coll
Editing: Eli F. Bleich
Cast: Ira Rubin, Sam DeFazio, Andrea Martin
Format/Duration: B/W, 16 mm blown up to 35 mm / 15 minutes

THE BIG SHAVE (1967)
Direction: Martin Scorsese
Screenplay: Martin Scorsese
Cinematography: Ares Demertzis
Cast: Peter Bernuth
Format/Duration: Color, 16 mm / 6 minutes

WHO'S THAT KNOCKING ON MY DOOR? (1969)
Production: Joseph Weill, Betzi and Haig Manoogian
Direction: Martin Scorsese
Screenplay: Martin Scorsese

Cinematography: Michael Wadleigh, Richard H. Coll, Max Fisher
Editing: Thelma Schoonmaker
Cast: Zina Bethune, Harvey Keitel
Format/Duration: Color, 35 mm / 90 minutes

BOXCAR BERTHA (1972)
Production: Roger Corman
Production Company: American International Pictures
Direction: Martin Scorsese
Screenplay: Joyce H. Corrington and John William
    Corrington
Cinematography: John Stephens
Editing: Buzz Feitshans
Music: Gib Builbeau, Thad Maxwell
Cast: Barbra Hershey, David Carradine
Format/Duration: Color, 35 mm / 93 minutes

MEAN STREETS (1973)
Production: Jonathan L. Taplin
Production Company: Warner Brothers
Direction: Martin Scorsese
Screenplay: Martin Scorsese and Mardik Martin
Cinematography: Kent Wakeford
Editing: Sid Levin
Cast: Robert De Niro, Harvey Keitel, David Proval
Format/Duration: Color, 35 mm / 110 minutes

ALICE DOESN'T LIVE HERE ANYMORE (1974)
Production: David Susskind and Audrey Maas
Production Company: Warner Brothers
Direction: Martin Scorsese
Screenplay: Robert Getchell
Cinematography: Kent Wakeford
Editing: Marcia Lucas
Music: Richard LaSalle
Cast: Ellen Burstyn, Kris Kristofferson, Harvey Keitel, Alfred Lutter
Format/Duration: Color, 35 mm / 111 minutes

ITALIANAMERICAN (1974)
Production: Elaine Attias, Saul Rubin
Production Company: National Communications Foundation
Direction: Martin Scorsese

Screenplay: Lawrence D. Cohen, Mardik Martin, Martin Scorsese
Cinematography: Alec Hirschfeld
Editing: Bert Lovitt
Format/Duration: Color, 35 mm / 48 minutes

TAXI DRIVER (1976)
Production: Michael and Julia Phillips
Production Company: Columbia
Direction: Martin Scorsese
Screenplay: Paul Schrader
Cinematography: Michael Chapman
Editing: Marcia Lucas, Tom Rolf, Melvin Shapiro
Music: Bernard Hermann
Cast: Robert De Niro, Cybill Shepherd, Jodie Foster, Harvey Keitel
Format/Duration: Color, 35 mm / 112 minutes

NEW YORK, NEW YORK (1977)
Production: Irwin Winkler and Robert Chartoff
Production Company: United Artists
Direction: Martin Scorsese
Screenplay: Earl Mac Rauch, Mardik Martin
Cinematography: Laszlo Kovacs
Editing: Irving Lerner, Marcia Lucas, Tom Rolf, B. Lovitt
Cast: Liza Minnelli, Robert De Niro
Format/Duration: Color, 35 mm / 137 minutes

THE LAST WALTZ (1978)
Production: Robbie Robertson
Production Company: United Artists
Direction: Martin Scorsese
Cinematography: Michael Chapman, Laszlo Kovacs, Vilmos Zsigmo,
    David Meyers, Bobby Byne, Michael Watkins, Hiro Narita
Editing: Yeu-Bun Yee, Jan Roblee
Format/Duration: Color, 35 mm / 119 minutes

AMERICAN BOY: A PROFILE OF STEVEN PRINCE (1978)
Production: Bert Lovitt, Jim Wheat, Ken Wheat
Direction: Martin Scorsese
Cinematography: Michael Chapman
Editing: Amy Jones, Bert Lovitt
Music: Neil Young
Format/Duration: Color, 35 mm / 55 minutes

RAGING BULL (1980)
Production: Robert Chartoff and Irwin Winkler
Production Company: United Artists
Direction: Martin Scorsese
Screenplay: Paul Shrader and Mardik Martin
Cinematography: Michael Chapman
Editing: Thelma Schoonmaker
Music: Pietro Mascagni
Cast: Robert De Niro, Joe Pesci, Cathy Moriarity
Format/Duration: B/W, 35 mm / 128 minutes

THE KING OF COMEDY (1982)
Production: Arnon Milchan
Production Company: Twentieth-Century Fox
Direction: Martin Scorsese
Cinematography: Fred Schuler
Editing: Thelma Schoonmaker
Music: Robbie Robertson
Cast: Robert De Niro, Jerry Lewis, Sandra Bernhard
Format/Duration: Color, 35 mm / 109 minutes

AFTER HOURS (1985)
Production: Amy Robinson, Griffin Dunne, Robert F. Colesberry
Production Company: Warner Brothers
Direction: Martin Scorsese
Screenplay: Joseph Minton
Cinematography: Michael Ballhaus
Editing: Thelma Schoonmaker
Music: Howard Shore
Cast: Griffin Dunne, Rosanna Arquette
Format/Duration: Color, 35 mm / 97 minutes

THE COLOR OF MONEY (1986)
Production: Irving Axelrad and Barbara De Fina
Production Company: Touchstone Pictures
Direction: Martin Scorsese
Screenplay: Richard Price
Cinematography: Michael Ballhaus
Editing: Thelma Schoonmaker
Music: Robbie Robertson

Cast: Paul Newman, Tom Cruise, Mary Elizabeth Mastrantonio
Format/Duration: Color, 35 mm / 117 minutes

THE LAST TEMPTATION OF CHRIST (1988)
Production: Barbara De Fina and Harry J. Ufland
Production Company: Universal Pictures
Direction: Martin Scorsese
Screenplay: Paul Schrader
Cinematography: Michael Ballhaus
Editing: Thelma Schoonmaker
Music: Peter Gabriel
Cast: Willem Dafoe, Harvey Keitel, Verna Bloom
Format/Duration: Color, 35 mm / 164 minutes

NEW YORK STORIES (SEGMENT ONE, "LIFE LESSONS") (1989)
Production: Barbara De Fina
Production Company: Touchstone Pictures
Direction: Martin Scorsese
Screenplay: Richard Price
Cinematography: Nestor Almendros
Editing: Thelma Schoonmaker
Music: Carmine Coppola, August Darnell
Cast: Nick Nolte, Rosanna Arquette
Format/Duration: Color, 35 mm / 120 minutes (entire film)

GOODFELLAS (1990)
Production: Barbara De Fina, Bruce S. Pustin, Irwin Winkler
Production Company: Warner Brothers
Direction: Martin Scorsese
Screenplay: Nicholas Pileggi and Martin Scorsese
Cinematography: Michael Ballhaus
Editing: Thelma Schoonmaker
Cast: Ray Liotta, Robert De Niro, Joe Pesci, Lorraine Bracco, Paul Sorvino
Format/Duration: Color, 35 mm / 146 minutes

CAPE FEAR (1991)
Production: Barbara De Fina, Kathleen Kennedy, Frank Marshall
Production Company: Tribeca Productions, Cappa Films, Amblin
    Entertainment, Universal Pictures
Direction: Martin Scorsese
Screenplay: Wesley Strick

Cinematography: Freddie Francis
Editing: Thelma Schoonmaker
Music: Elmer Bernstein
Cast: Robert De Niro, Nick Nolte, Jessica Lange, Juliette Lewis
Format/Duration: Color, 35 mm / 128 minutes

THE AGE OF INNOCENCE (1993)
Production: Barbara De Fina, Bruce S. Pustin, Joseph P. Reidy
Production Company: Columbia Pictures
Direction: Martin Scorsese
Screenplay: Jay Cocks and Martin Scorsese
Cinematography: Michael Ballhaus
Editing: Thelma Schoonmaker
Music: Elmer Bernstein
Cast: Daniel Day-Lewis, Michelle Pfeiffer, Winona Ryder
Format/Duration: Color, 35 mm / 139 minutes

CASINO (1995)
Production: Barbara De Fina, Joseph P. Reidy Production Company,
    De Fina-Cappa, Syalis D. A. & Legende Enterprises, Universal Pictures
Direction: Martin Scorsese
Screenplay: Nicholas Pileggi and Martin Scorsese
Cinematography: Robert Richardson
Editing: Thelma Schoonmaker
Cast: Robert De Niro, Sharon Stone, Joe Pesci
Format/Duration: Color, 35 mm / 177 minutes

**A PERSONAL JOURNEY THROUGH AMERICAN MOVIES
WITH MARTIN SCORSESE** (1995)
Production: Florence Dauman, British Film Institute (BFI),
    Miramax Films
Direction: Martin Scorsese, Michael Henry Wilson
Screenplay: Martin Scorsese, Michael Henry Wilson
Cinematography: Jean-Yves Escoffier, Frances Reid, Nancy Schreiber
Editing: Kenneth Levis, David Lindblom
Cast: Martin Scorsese
Format/Duration: Black and White, Color / 225 minutes

KUNDUN (1998)
Production: Barbara De Fina, Laura Fattori, Scott Harris,
    Melissa Mathison

Production Company: Walt Disney Productions, Refuge Productions,
   De Fine-Cappa, Touchstone Pictures
Direction: Martin Scorsese
Screenplay: Melissa Mathison
Cinematography: Roger Deakins
Editing: Thelma Schoonmaker
Music: Philip Glass
Cast: Tenzin Thuthob Tsarong, Gyurme Tetho Tulku, Jamyang
   Kinga Tenzin
Format/Duration: Color, 35 mm / 134 minutes

BRINGING OUT THE DEAD (1999)
Production: Barbara De Fina, Scott Rudin
Production Company: Paramount Pictures, Touchstone Pictures
   Direction, Martin Scorsese
Screenplay: Paul Schrader
Cinematography: Robert Richardson
Editing: Thelma Schoonmaker
Music: Elmer Bernstein
Cast: Nicolas Cage, Patricia Arquette, John Goodman, Ving Rhames,
   Tom Sizemore
Format/Duration: Color, 35 mm / 121 minutes

IL MIO VIAGGIO IN ITALIA (1999)
Production: Giorgio Armani, Barbara De Fina, Giuliana Del Punta,
   Bruno Restuccia, Cappa Production, Meditrade, Paso Doble Film
Direction: Martin Scorsese
Screenplay: Suso Cecchi d'Amico, Raffaele Donato, Kent Jones,
   Martin Scorsese
Cinematography: Phil Abraham, William Rexer
Editing: Thelma Schoonmaker
Cast: Martin Scorsese
Format/Duration: Black and White, Color / 246 minutes

GANGS OF NEW YORK (2002)
Production: Alberto Grimaldi, Harvey Weinstein
Production Company: Miramax Films, Initial Entertainment Group
Direction: Martin Scorsese
Screenplay: Jay Cocks, Steven Zaillian, Kenneth Lonergan
Cinematography: Michael Ballhaus
Editing: Thelma Schoonmaker

Music: Bono, Adam Clayton, Peter Gabriel, Larry Mullen Jr.,
    Jocelyn Pook, Howard Shore, The Edge
Cast: Leonardo DiCaprio, Daniel Day-Lewis, Cameron Diaz,
    Jim Broadbent, Henry Thomas, Liam Neeson
Format/Duration: Color, 35 mm / 167 min.

THE BLUES (EPISODE, "FEEL LIKE GOING HOME") (2003)
Production: Martin Scorsese, Samuel D. Pollard
Production Company: Vulcan Productions
Direction: Martin Scorsese
Screenplay: Peter Guralnick
Cinematography: Arthur Jafa
Editing: David Tedeschi
Music and Cast: Corey Harris, John Lee Hooker, Son House, Salif Keita,
    Taj Mahal, Ali Farke Touré, Muddy Waters
Format: Color, 35 mm

Selected Bibliography

Ackroyd, Peter. "All the Rage." *Spectator*, 28 February 1981, 26.

Barton, Carlin A. "The Scandal of the Arena." *Representations* 27 (1989): 1–36.

Blake, Richard A. "Redeemed in Blood: The Sacramental Universe of Martin Scorsese." *Journal of Popular Film and Television* 24 (1996): 2–9.

Boyum, Joy Gould. "A Work of Power and Distinction." *Wall Street Journal*, 28 November 1980, 11.

Brunette, Peter, ed. *Martin Scorsese: Interviews*. Jackson: University Press of Mississippi, 1999.

Coleman, John. "Box and Cocks." *New Statesman*, 20 February 1981, 23.

Cook, Pam. "Masculinity in Crisis?: Pam Cook on Tragedy and Identification in *Raging Bull*." *Screen* 23 (1982): 39–46.

Dickstein, Morris. "Self-Tormentors." *Partisan Review* 64 (1994): 658–664.

Friedman, Lawrence S. *The Cinema of Martin Scorsese*. New York: Continuum, 1998.

Girgus, Sam B. *America on Film: Modernism, Documentary, and a Changing America*. New York: Cambridge University Press, 2002.

Grindon, Leger. "Body and Soul: The Structure of Meaning in the Boxing Film Genre." *Cinema Journal* 35 (1996): 54–69.

Halberstam, Judith. *Female Masculinity*. Durham: Duke University Press, 1998.

Hemmeter, Gail Garnicelli, and Thomas Hemmeter. "The Word Made Flesh: Language in Raging Bull." *Literature/Film Quarterly* 14 (1986): 101–105.

Johnson, Carol Siri. "Constructing Machismo in *Mean Streets* and *Raging Bull*." *Perspectives on Raging Bull*, ed. Steven G. Kellman. New York: G. K. Hall, 1994, 96–106.

Kael, Pauline. "Religious Pulp, or The Incredible Hulk." *New Yorker*, 8 December 1980, 217–225.

Kellman, Steven G., ed. *Perspectives on Raging Bull*. New York: G. K. Hall, 1994.

Keyser, Lester J. *Martin Scorsese*. New York: Twayne, 1992.

La Motta, Jake, Joseph Carter, and Peter Savage. *Raging Bull*. 1970. Reprinted. New York: Bantam, 1980.

Leed, Barry H. "Scorsese vs. Mailer: Boxing as Redemption in *Raging Bull* and *An American Dream.*" *Perspectives on Raging Bull*, ed. Steven G. Kellman. New York: G. K. Hall, 1994, 131–135.

Librach, Ronald S. "The Last Temptation in Mean Streets and Raging Bull." *Literature/Film Quarterly* 20 (1992): 14–24.

Malcolm, Derek. "The Punch in Scorsese's Ring Cycle." *Guardian*, 14 February 1981, 10.

Mortimer, Barbara. "Portraits of the Postmodern Person in *Taxi Driver, Raging Bull,* and *The King of Comedy.*" *Journal of Film and Video* 49 (1997): 28–38.

Nicholls, Mark. "Something For the Man Who Has Everything: Melancholia and the Films of Martin Scorsese." *Playing the Man: New Approaches to Masculinity*, eds. Dave Trudinger, Katherine Biber, and Tom Sear. Annandale, Australia: Pluto Press, 1999, 39–51, 215–216.

Nicholls, Mark. *Scorsese's Men: Melancholia and the Mob*. Annandale, Australia: Pluto Press, 2004.

O'Toole, Lawrence. "Going the Distance, and Much, Much Farther." *Maclean's*, 1 December 1980, p. 73.

Ringel, Eleanor. "*Raging Bull* Goes the Distance in Spite of Itself." *Atlanta Constitution*, 20 February 1981, 3B.

Thompson, David, and Ian Christie, eds. *Scorsese on Scorsese*. London: Faber and Faber, 1989.

Tomasulo, Frank P. "Raging Bully: Postmodern Violence and Masculinity in *Raging Bull.*" *Mythologies of Violence in Postmodern Media*, ed. Christopher Sharrett. Detroit: Wayne State University Press, 1999, 175–197.

Westerbeck, Colin L., Jr. "Shadowboxing: A Fighter's Stance toward Life." *Commonweal*, 16 January 1981, pp. 20–21.

Weiss, Marion W. "Linguistic Coding in the Films of Martin Scorsese." *Semiotica* 55 (1985): 185–194.

Index